Janet Thomson Hamilton

Poems and Ballads

Janet Thomson Hamilton

Poems and Ballads

ISBN/EAN: 9783337370084

Printed in Europe, USA, Canada, Australia, Japan

Cover: Foto ©Thomas Meinert / pixelio.de

More available books at **www.hansebooks.com**

POEMS AND BALLADS.

Second Edition.

BY

JANET HAMILTON,

AUTHORESS OF "POEMS AND ESSAYS," AND " POEMS AND SKETCHES."

WITH INTRODUCTORY PAPERS BY THE REV. GEORGE GILFILLAN
AND THE REV. ALEXANDER WALLACE, D.D.

GLASGOW:

JAMES MACLEHOSE, 61 ST. VINCENT STREET.

1873.

This Volume

Ah, not low my aspirations, Upward to the heaven above us,
 High and strong my soul's desire, Onward in the march of mind :
To assist my toiling brothers Upward, to the shrine of freedom.
 Upward, onward to aspire.   Onward, working for our kind.

   This to you, my working brothers,
    I inscribe ; may nothing low
   Dwell in mind, in heart, or habit ;
    Upward look, and onward go !

PREFATORY NOTE.

THE Introductory Paper prefixed to this volume from the pen of the Rev. George Gilfillan, of Dundee, with the addition of a paper descriptive of a visit to the Authoress "at her ain fireside," by the Rev. Alex. Wallace, D.D., Glasgow, preclude the necessity of any lengthened prefatory address from me; and I shall only say that in offering this Second Edition of "POEMS AND BALLADS" to the public, I have been induced to do so on account of having had a number of enquiries for it, which could not be answered, owing to the edition having been out of print within a few months after it was published, five years ago, and I hope this second edition will meet with the same kind and generous reception which was awarded to the first.

I trust I shall be pardoned in saying here, that for the last five years I have been entirely blind, and for three years past have been all but wholly confined to bed, my son and daughter having to lift me out for an hour or two when my strength will admit of it. I trust no one will think that this is written in a murmuring or complaining spirit. Not so. I thank God every day that my husband

and myself are still in the land of the living, which my friends will think we have good cause to do when they are told that we have now entered on our sixty-fifth year of married life.

Sincerely hoping my egotism in this will be excused, and as, in the common course of nature, I must be nearing " the silent land, which gives back no echo to the world again." I would once more (seeing it may be the last time) return my sincere thanks to my friends, the press and the public, for the genial reception my literary efforts received from them, and shall conclude with a stanza from one of my own poems, which is exceedingly appropriate in my present condition :—

> " I am now an aged worker;
> I have toiled, and read, and sung;
> Oft my lyre was tuned to gladness,
> Ah ! more oft by woe unstrung.
> Now my toils are nearly ended,
> And my song ere long shall cease,
> Day is waning, shadows falling,
> Soon my eyes shall close in peace."

JANET HAMILTON
LANGLOAN COATBRIDGE

May, 1873.

CONTENTS.

CONTENTS.

Thy ready hand I still could claim
in every change of life the same
when burning shame and bitter grief
assailed my heart my best relief
next to my god in thee i found
no balm no sure to heal the wound
than thy kind words and truthful love
no false or cruel tongue could move
thy steadfast mind or make thee falter
in dutys path—upon the altar
of holy faith and christian love
thou laidst thy heart—may god above
this choicest blessings daily shed
on thy beloved and duteous head—

JANET HAMILTON

The following is a Copy of the foregoing Lines.

Thy ready hand I still could claim,
In every change of life the same:
When burning shame and bitter grief
Assailed my heart, my best relief,
Next to my God, in thee I found.
No balm so sure to heal the wound
Than thy kind words, and truthful love.

No false or cruel tongue could move
Thy steadfast mind, or make thee falter
In duty's path. Upon the altar
Of holy faith and Christian love
Thou laidst thy heart. May God above
His choicest blessings daily shed
On thy beloved and duteous head!

JANET HAMILTON

JANET HAMILTON:

HER LIFE AND POETICAL CHARACTER.

--------·•·--------

GREAT and rapid as the march of the higher culture
has been and is, it is gratifying to know that it has
not yet been able to extinguish the race of self-taught
authors, nor to eliminate those elements of simplicity
and sturdy common sense which, along with native
genius, have formed the staple of their character and
the inspiration of their works. It is as in nature.
While cultivation has turned so many parts of the
country into gardens, and gardens into Edens, and made
even graveyards blossom as the rose, it has not extir-
pated the wild brier in the lanes, and still permits
the heather to bloom, and the canna to wave upon a
thousand hills. And so mental culture has not yet
succeeded, nor we trust ever shall, in producing that
monotonous table-land level in which all is equally

B

lofty, and equally conventional and dull, in which
there is left no room for the play of untaught power,
and in which the triumph of art has deadened the
"lustihood of nature." Still, ever and anon, into the
full blaze of the nineteenth century, come out such

> " Birds of the wilderness,
> Blithesome and cumberless,"

as Hugh Miller, Alexander Smith, and the subject of
the following sketch, that remarkable woman, JANET
HAMILTON.

Self-teaching is unquestionably fraught with advantages for which no amount of culture can compensate.
Its source being the soul, it is obvious that the self-
educated person has the privilege of coming more
directly in contact with that interior light. Far more
than the highly-cultured man, he is alone with his
own spirit, and realizes it almost as a divine presence
within him. In this we may seem to be recording
the experiences of all gifted souls, whether educated
or not. But, probably, in the case of Shakspeare and
Bunyan, for instance, this impression may have been
stronger and more palpable than in that of more
refined but artificial spirits. And perhaps Gray,
in his "Progress of Poesy," alludes to this direct

communion with ideal truth and beauty on the part
of the inspired boy of Avon, when he sings—

    " Far from the sun and summer gale,
      In thy green lap was Nature's darling laid,
      What time, where lucid Avon strayed,
      To him the Mighty Mother did unveil
      Her awful face : the dauntless child
      Stretched forth his little arms and smiled."

Yes ! the long, long golden dream of Bunyan, and the
two transcendent visions of Burns—the one in the
Auld Clay Biggin', and the other by the roofless wa's
of Lincluden Abbey—were never, could never, have
been dreamed or imagined by scholars or Professors
in College Halls. The dungeon, or the hovel, is a
fitter atmosphere for the higher order of imagination, when that exists, than the library of the British
Museum, or the drawing-room in Buckingham Palace,
or even in Balmoral ; and although Solomon tells us
that the spider taketh hold with her hands in king's
palaces, the spirit of genius is more chary of its
presence, and seeks rather the woodland cottage, or
the shieling on the mountain side. Courts rarely rear
a great thinker or poet. Often men of true original
power have found, or forced, their way into them ;
but often, too, they have exclaimed in disgust or
scorn, " Let us away, this is no place for us ; since

being honest we say what we believe, and since being
gifted with native insight we say what others do *not*
believe, because they are unable to see." A highly-
cultured mind, unless singularly original, sits under
the conflicting lights and shadows of a thousand
authors, as under the trees of a wide wind-swept
forest. The self-taught man or woman of genius sits
under the stern one light, or one stern shadow of his
own purpose and ideal.

The self-taught have usually greater freshness of
feeling in beholding Nature, and a keener sympathy
with men, than the better instructed. Having read
fewer descriptions, they look at the thing described
more exactly as it is. Many see not Nature's thunder-
storm, but Thomson's or Byron's; not Bruar-water
itself, but Burns' picture of it; Scott's Trossachs, not
the beautiful place itself; and hence, often when they
try to describe such scenes, they merely dilute the
descriptions of others, and produce shadows of shades.
The self-taught simply record the contact between
their own genius and Nature's works. Shakspeare
paints the brook in "Hamlet," and the forest in "As
You Like it;" and Burns the linn, in "Hallowe'en,"
from their own eyesight, and as if there had not
been another poet in the world. James Hogg, in

" Kilmeny," is thinking of no scene but that glen winding up between the dark hills of Abruchil and the fairy environs of Duniera, where lay the path of his heroine,

> " To meet the visions of celestial day."

Hugh Miller, looking at Ben Wyvis, is not dreaming of Alpine raptures in Byron, or Grampian raptures in Christopher North, but simply of the huge hoary mountain of his own native strath. Janet Hamilton does not sing of hills she has never seen unless in picture or poem, but of what has met her own eye—

> " A lanely loch, a muirland broon,
>   A warl o' whins and heather ;
> Whaur aft when life was young I strayed
>   The berries blae to gather.

> " Sae bonnie bloomed the gowden broom,
>   Sae green the feathery bracken,
> An' rosy brier, dear to my een,
>   Ere licht had them forsaken."

And thus all self-taught genius retains more than the other the freshness of the feelings with which the child sees and returns in vivid photograph the glories of the universe ; and so, in reference to humanity, the self-taught have not only

> " Gazed at Nature's naked loveliness,"

but have seen man, too, stripped of all the dress of conventionalism, in his original strength and weakness, in his merits and faults, and have profited by the sight, and found it, through familiarity, not so disenchanting as is sometimes supposed. No one can be so thoroughly up to the middle or higher classes as a self-taught genius is to the lower, for the simple reason that the lower classes have far less disguise, especially from one of themselves, and he sees what Lear calls " unaccom- modated man"—man almost savage indeed, but with a strange aboriginal light, as if from Preadamite days, glimmering around him. Hence Burns, conversant as he was with the sins and miseries of his own rank, could, in his walk with Dugald Stewart alongst the summit of the Braid hills, when he beheld a hundred smoking cottages, think only of the worth, honesty, and happiness which he knew such humble roofs con- cealed. And so, although Janet Hamilton is a stern limner of the evils of intemperance, as she has seen it destroying the virtues and withering the manhood of so many of the poor, yet she does full and heaped-up justice to the manhood and the excellence which are so recklessly ruined thereby. Few self-taught authors have been misanthropes—and this because, first, the near and habitual sight of man, even in his lowest degradation, generates a calm, contemplative spirit in the wise observer, rather than scorn—sorrow more than anger; because, again, he remarks the great pro-portion of good which mingles with the evil; and because, thirdly, he sees among the humble less of that deceit and falsehood which constitute, so to speak, the Devil department in the race, and which culture and civilization, in themselves, serve rather to foster than to extirpate.

The self-taught strugglers with narrow circumstances learn usually a certain hardihood of spirit, a contempt for petty difficulties and for puling sentimentalisms. They are often of an iron mould, not used to the melt-ing mood, and sometimes a little impatient of the sensitive and the weak among whom they mingle. They have often a hatred at the fantastic, the lacka-daisical, and the mystical. This they contract by dealing with hard, harsh, practical results. We see not a little of this in the writings, as well as in the history of Janet Hamilton. Belonging, though she does, to the softer sex, she displays a manlike purpose, a rugged independence of spirit, and a contempt for all "mealy-mouthedness" and gilded humbug, which make her seem almost an incarnation of the better nature of Burns. It is with real sorrows, the sufferings of Italian prisoners, the miseries of the drunkard's family, the baffled aspirations of the hero and the patriot, the Mazzini and the Garibaldi, that honest Janet sympathises; not with the sentimental pangs of love-sick young ladies, or the pathetic yearnings of fame-seeking and moustache-sporting young men. She never forgets that there was a time when, newly married, all her and her husband's fortune was a single Spanish dollar! She has wrestled with the real evils, the serpents of poverty and want, and strangled them almost in her cradle, and cares little for the dust blown by the wings of butterflies, or the stings inflicted by the mouths of gadflies. She feels for real calamities, but laughs at small annoyances, and at those who parade them. And now, under the privation of total blindness, she is discovering a "silent magnanimity" which shows a noble nature; and when she speaks out her sorrow, it is in language as patient and dignified as it is musical and powerful.

The self-taught are emphatically men of one book. Hall said of Dr. Kippis, "that though he was naturally a clever man, he laid so many books upon his brains that they could not move"—like a little emmet burdened with a piece of plaster ten times its own size! Few self-taught men lay such loads upon their minds. To them, having few books, but being intimately acquainted with what they have, no book is a burden, but each book rather (as in that clever paper of Washington Irving, entitled the "Art of Bookmaking") may be compared to a garment, or piece of armour put on, fitted to the size and shape of the wearer, and forwarding, instead of retarding, his movements. One man of this class masters his Bible, as Bunyan did, and the book becomes to him a coat of mail; another Shakspeare, and he who has mastered the world's master walks gowned and swelling in a magnificent and flowing style of speech ; a third Euclid, and it, as with James Fergusson and other self-taught men of science, is transformed into a pair of iron-spiked shoes to convey them up the steep and rugged paths of natural philosophy; a fourth, the ballad poetry of Scotland, and, lo ! it becomes the guid braid bonnet on the swarthy brow of a Burns ; and a fifth, like Cobbett, the "Tale of a Tub," and it becomes a sharp scimitar glittering with poison, and helping him to clear his wild Ishmaelitish way and do his destructive work. "Beware the man of one book," is a true as well as an old saying. Hugh Miller, for instance, had made Cowper, Shenstone, Young, and other classics his own in boyhood, and they gave a masculine tinge to his thought and style

ever afterwards.   Alexander Smith was quite steeped
in Chaucer, Spenser, Shelley, and Keats; and Janet
Hamilton owns her early obligations to Milton, Burns,
Ramsay, Fergusson, the *Spectator*, and the *Rambler*,
books which she did not glance at hurriedly or dandle
over like girls of the present day, but at once devoured
rapidly at first, and often recurred to, and long and
thoroughly digested.

In Janet's poems, as well as prose writings, we see
evidences of the advantage she has derived from her
want of early opportunities, although, of course, she
displays, too, some of the drawbacks of the self-taught
—the want of width and variety of view, that polish
and correctness which only a classical education can
bestow, and exhibits a little of that opinionativeness
and dogmatism which spring partly from the clearness
and strength of their mental vision, and partly from
their mingling so much with their inferiors.   Sometimes she resembles her class in this—that seeing a
subject so intensely themselves, they have little patience
with those who cannot, though they would, behold it
at the same angle—just as we have known lynx-eyed
persons getting excessively wroth with their short-
sighted brethren for not observing certain minute or
distant points in a landscape.   But, after making all

deductions, the works of this remarkable woman are productions of uncommon excellence, discovering grasp of intellect, vividness of fancy, a "carlstalk" of common sense, intelligent decisiveness of view, power, facility— on the whole, correctness, and sometimes even elevation of language.

We have called her a remarkable woman ; and she is so, because she combines many of the characteristics of a heroine and an author in humble life—the energy of will and strength of character marking the one, with the freshness, originality, and simple sinewy vigour of the other.   A glance at her life may fitly precede a brief estimate of her works.

She was born in the parish of Shotts, Lanarkshire, in October, 1795.   October, her native, has always continued her favourite month, and some of the sweetest verses in the present volume are devoted to the mild glories, the drooping honours, the mellow calm, the rich colours, and the pensive charm of that last month of the most delightful season of the year.   Carshill was the name of the clachan where she was born. Her maiden name was Janet Thomson, and through her maternal ancestors she was connected with the children of the Covenant.   She is the fifth in descent from John Whitelaw, Stand, Monkland, who was executed at the Old Tolbooth of Edinburgh, 1683, four years after the battle at Bothwell Bridge, in which he had taken a part, and was otherwise well known as a determined supporter of Covenanting principles. Her mother's name was Mary Brownlee, and her grandfather was a very remarkable person in his day. Our readers, by turning to her volume, entitled "Poems and Sketches," p. 170, will find a lengthened and very interesting account of Old Brownlee, who seems to have been in reality very nearly what David Deans was in fiction, or the "Cottar of the Saturday Night" in poetry. The whole chapter, entitled "Scottish Life and Character," might almost have appeared in Wilson's "Lights and Shadows," and shows a kindred keenness of eye in hitting off the peculiarities and the stalwart virtues of the old types of Scottish character.

We give, in her own words, a portion of her early reminiscences :—" My father, being bred a shoemaker, found it convenient to remove to the town of Hamilton with his wife and child (myself). I would then be between two and three years of age. There we resided till I was about seven years old, when my parents, having suffered severely in their health by the close confinement, removed to the small village of Langloan, parish of Old Monkland, where they both worked as

field labourers on the home farm of the estate of Drumpellier for about two years, while I kept house at
home ; and being early taught by my mother to spin,
my daily task, in her absence, was to produce two hanks
of sale yarn, in which I seldom failed. When my
mother left the out-door labour I was taught to work
at the tambour-frame, which was then a very remu-
nerative employment for women and girls. My father
also left the out-door labour a short time after, and
commenced working at his trade on his own account.
He engaged a very respectable young man to assist
him in his work. This young man became my husband
in 1809. I had ten children by him, seven of whom,
with their father, still survive. We have lived to-
gether in the married state for 59 years. My husband
will be eighty years of age in August, 1868, and I
seventy-three in October of the same year."

She says again—"Two little incidents I will relate
here. The one refers to the marriage of my parents.
They were proclaimed in the Kirk of Shotts, and
from thence went on foot to Glasgow, and were married by a Dr. Pirie, of what denomination I do not
know." [He was a Burgher, and predecessor of Dr.
Dick, Professor of Theology in the Secession Hall.]
"The other includes some little incidents of my own

marriage. We started on foot early for Glasgow, on a cold February morning, in the year 1809. We went to the house of an acquaintance of my husband, and told him we had come to be married. He sent his porter to the Rev. Dr. Lockhart, of College Church, the late county M.P.'s father, who asked if we had any one to witness the marriage. Our answer was in the negative. The porter and Betty, the housemaid, were called in to witness—the knot was tied, which has never yet been loosed. I never saw the Doctor's face, and I can pass my word he never saw mine. We then returned to the friend's house, got some refreshment, took the road home again on foot, arrived after dark, got in unperceived by any of my girlish companions, had a cup of tea with a few of the old neighbours, and at the breakfast table next morning we took stock of our worldly gear. Our humble household plenishing was all paid, and my husband had a Spanish dollar, and on that and our two pair of hands we started, and though many battles and bustles have had to be encountered, with the help of a good and kind God, we have always been able to keep the wolf from the door."

In company with our excellent friend, Wm. Logan, of Glasgow, we visited the interesting old couple in

December, 1866, and were greatly delighted on the one hand with the appearance of the husband, so hale and strong for his years—his cheek ruddy, his nerve firm, and his reverence and love for his wife unbounded ; and, on the other, with Janet's calm, commanding aspect—her clear and correct enunciation—as if (to use Scott's expression) "she spoke from a prent book" —the generous and noble sentiments she uttered on many subjects introduced—the fluency and emphasis with which she repeated a poem of her own, some one hundred lines long—and the dignity with which she was evidently bearing the great calamity of blindness. We thought involuntarily of that striking character in the Bride of Lammermoor—blind old Alice —whose sense, shrewdness, and majesty of bearing were such, that people who did not know her could hardly believe she was blind, and almost trembled in her presence, as if her sightless orbs and lofty forehead were full of essential and inevitable vision. We shall never forget the glowing enthusiasm with which Janet spoke of our hero Garibaldi, and of the cause of Italian freedom in general. Her blindness and her genius combined suggested many a memory—of worthy Dr. Blacklock, the kind-hearted patron of Burns ; of Frances Brown, the blind Irish poetess ; of Milton

himself. and of those great ancient bards of whom
he sings (although Janet would be the last in her true
modesty to wish to be compared for power to such
Titans of the race) :—

> " Nor sometimes forget
> Those other two equalled with me in fate,
> So were I equalled with them in renown—
> Blind Thamyris and blind Mæonides,
> And Tiresias and Phineas, prophets old."

We left altogether with very peculiar emotions, and
the memory of our visit to Langloan shall not soon be
forgotten.

In the preface to the second edition of her Poems
and Essays, Mrs. Hamilton has given a brief but
pleasing sketch of her young studies ; her early mastery
of the alphabet; her reading of Bible stories and
children's halfpenny books ere she was five years of
age ; her finding, when eight, upon the loom of an
intellectual weaver, a copy of Paradise Lost and Allan
Ramsay's poems ; her becoming a reader in the village
library, where she had access to many good and solid
books, in history, geography, biography, travels, and
voyages; her devouring, instead of novels, of which
she met few, Rollin, Plutarch's Lives, Ancient Universal History, Raynal's India, and Pitscottie's Scotland,
besides the *Spectator*, *Rambler*, Fergusson, Burns, and

Macneill, as tidbits, while all the time she had a daily task assigned her—never neglected—first at the spinning wheel, and afterwards at the tambouring frame. Her mother, who was a very pious woman, made her read a chapter from the Bible every morning, and this practice, she says, was never omitted for a single day till she married and left the house; and "during all the years of childhood, every night when I laid my head on my pillow my mother's mouth was close at my ear praying for me, and teaching me to pray for myself."

After her marriage, when engaged in rearing a young family on small means, her reading hours were taken from her sleep, and many an hour she spent in this way, holding the book in one hand and nursing an infant on her lap with the other. In a MS. which lies before us, she gives an interesting account of the manner in which she taught her own children to read. She began to teach every one of them to read and spell when they attained the age of five years. They were taught the alphabet and small words from the beginning of the Assembly's Shorter Catechism. That was the only spelling book she ever used. The first lesson in reading she gave them was the first chapter of St. John's Gospel, with the beginning of the Book of

Genesis.   She describes very picturesquely her appearance while engaged in teaching her children.   "The whole of the lessons were given by me when busy at the tambour frame, and the little urchin standing with book in hand beside me, and oftentimes his clothes had many patches and some rents in them, and perhaps not over clean a face, being recently employed in doing some of the duties of the housemaid, for the boys as well as the girls had to perform these duties as they grew up, till they were old enough to commence to learn trades."   In this way she made them good scholars, and what was better, obedient children, and, on the whole, useful and respectable members of society.

While thus employed in instructing her children she persevered, amid all discouragements, with her own self-culture.   She often tells how for years she got the loan of *Blackwood*, and, whilst nursing her child, she would take the magazine out from a sort of hole in the wall, and if any one unexpectedly entered the house she quickly replaced it, as if afraid of its being known.   She did the same with Shakspeare and other noted authors, against whom in Scottish country circles there lingered then a prejudice which it was wiser to evade than to defy.

She began rather early to compose verses, and had, when between seventeen and nineteen years of age, produced about twenty pieces in rhyme, all of a strictly religious character; but after she had her third child, she did not indite a line till about the age of fifty-four, when she commenced writing for Cassells' "Working Man's Friend." It must be noticed that she could not write herself till about this age!*

Principal Robertson remarks, that Burns' prose compositions, with all their faults, were, considering his opportunities, more remarkable than even his poems. And the same holds true of Janet Hamilton's prose writings. For sound, solid sense, discrimination of character, and language clear, fluent, strong, and generally correct, they no less, or perhaps even more than her poems, testify to her remarkable powers, and are calculated to recommend her writings to that large class who have no taste for poetry.

The volume now in the reader's hands is, of course, of various and unequal merit. It consists of occasional poems on public events, particular deaths, etc.; of descriptive pieces, of moral poems, and of tales and legends. All possess an interest of their own, and will

---

* A facsimile of her very peculiar and self-invented handwriting is given elsewhere.

attract each its own class of admirers. Those burning
with political fervour will like her Garibaldian out-
pourings. Those whose passion is natural scenery
will delight in her fine strains on Spring and October,
now, alas! shadowed by the fact that these beauties no
more

> " Revisit now her eyes, which roll in vain
> To find the day."

Those who are either teetotalers, or sympathise
with Janet's intense hatred at whisky, will own that
she expresses that detestation with the utmost
eloquence, as well as sincerity. And those who like
the action still more than the word in poetry will
revel in her simple stories of Scottish life, expressing,
like the songs of Wordsworth's "Highland Reaper"—

> " Some natural sorrow, loss, or pain,
> That has been, and may be again."

In all these departments Janet is more or less
mistress, and that not so much from originality or
splendour of genius, as from the simplicity and
sincerity which stamp her poetry, like herself, " a
true thing."

With all those who know Janet Hamilton there
rests the impression not only that she has extraordinary
powers, and deserves to rank with the principal self-

taught poets of Scotland, but that above even this her moral nature towers distinguished. She is eminent for her high sense of honour and independence. She scorns everything mean, dastardly, false, and deceitful.

In her Christianity she is thoroughly sincere, and Catholic in spirit, although attached from principle, as well as from old association, to the Church of Scotland. Her father was an ardent reformer even when that cause was unpopular, and Janet has ever taken a deep interest in the affairs of the nation, especially on public questions affecting the moral welfare and eleva-tion of the people. Even still she must have her daily paper read to her, and in all foreign questions she continues to take especial interest.

The late Dr. Campbell, of the *British Standard*, knew Janet well, and used to say that " she had not only a firm and intelligent opinion of her own on most great public questions, but was, especially on Italian and Hungarian topics, better *posted-up* than most people."

One element of interest certainly attaches to the pre-sent volume. It is the author's last, or, as she calls it in the interesting MS. already more than once referred to, "the Benjamin of her pen." May that Benjamin never become the "Benoni," the child of her scrrow! May it meet with the generous reception with which her former productions were welcomed! We could take the somewhat lower ground of commending it as the production of a senior of seventy-three, never gifted with educational or conventional advantages, and now laden with the double burden of blindness and years. But we prefer to rest its claims upon its own literary merit, which is great, and upon the character of its author, which is nobler still.

GEORGE GILFILLAN.

DUNDEE, *1st September, 1868.*

JANET HAMILTON AT HER "AIN FIRESIDE."

By ALEXANDER WALLACE, D.D., Glasgow,

Author of " The Bible and Working People;" " The Desert and the Holy Land," etc.

FEW places could be more unfavourable for the cultivation of the poetic faculty than the smoky region in which the rapidly growing town of Coatbridge is situated, with its flaming furnaces and great mounds of slag, turning the green fields and the blessed light of heaven into a very pandemonium, and making confusion worse confounded, both above and below the vexed earth. Burns was born amid scenes of such rural loveliness, on the banks "o' bonnie Doon," that the most prosaic visitor to that classic spot would admit at once it was the fitting home of a poet, and quite worthy of being named any day along with "Dove's Nest," "Rydal Mount," and all the other romantic dwellings of the Lake poets; but the very idea of Coatbridge being the haunt of the muses seems to be utterly out of harmony with all their supposed parti-

ality for certain highly-favoured spots where there is a
rare combination of the beauties of nature. The muse
seems to have been more accommodating of late to the
stern necessities of the times; and so Ebenezer Elliot
hammers out his burning thoughts on his ringing anvil
at Sheffield, and David Wingate sings his exquisite
songs at the bottom of a coal pit, the dark sides of
which he has made radiant with the pure and tender
love of Uncle Reuben for Annie Weir. Tannahill
weaves his sweet Doric lays at the loom, and Janet
Hamilton, upwards of seventy years of age, and who
has never been at any school, touches the trembling
strings of the wild Scottish lyre, in her humble
dwelling at Langloan, and makes the roughest
denizen of that rough and fiery district proud of her
name. The Scottish muse found Burns at the plough,
when turning over the "wee, modest, crimson tippet
flower," and once more she has shown that there is no
royal road, no beaten tract on which to strew her gifts,
for "she threw her inspiring mantle" round Janet, at
the spinning wheel and the tambour frame, and in
the sooty region which the venerable poetess has
graphically described in the poem entitled "Oor
Location."

Lately we found ourselves threading our way through

this " mottie, misty clime," our object being to visit
this remarkable woman (take her all in all, the most
remarkable woman perhaps now living in Scotland),
of whom we had heard so much. Several times we
inquired the way to her dwelling, not that it was so
difficult to find, but we were curious to see how her
name would be received, and on every occasion 'the
very mention of it produced a pleasant smile on the
face of every one whom we questioned. All seemed
proud of "Old Janet," as they kindly named her.
Some gave her the familiar name of " Jenny," and
with a softer and more reverential tone than usual.
Our last inquiry was addressed to a rough-looking
fellow seated at a door-step, and who was doubtless
employed in some department of the Iron Works in
the district. He rose to his feet on hearing our
question, took the cutty pipe from his mouth, told us
that we had but to turn the corner, which he pointed
out, and go up a back stair. His face relaxed into a
smile, which was worth far more than his whole week's
earnings, as he closed his instructions with the assurance
that we would be certain to find Janet at home, as she
never left the house, and that she was " gey frail and
blin'." Pleased at the interest manifested in the
object of our visit by this rough diamond, we turned

the corner as directed and got into a collier-row
looking range of houses, with the usual number of ash-
pits. Women folk and childern were squatted about
the door-steps. Ascending the back stair, we found
the door open, and recognised Janet at once by her
peculiar head-dress covering her eyes, from which sight
has entirely fled. Most kindly did she welcome us to
her humble dwelling, which consists of two apartments,
a small kitchen, and a still smaller room entering from
it,—in short, a *"but and a ben."* Of course we must
retire to the best room, and there we could not fail to
observe one of the old-fashioned kind of cupboards or
ambries, a chest of drawers, and a small book-case, con-
taining a choice collection of books, several of which
were presents. One of these was shown us with no
small degree of pride, because a gift from a distinguished
officer who had fought side by side with Garibaldi in
his struggles for freedom. She referred with deep
emotion to a visit which one of the General's sons
had lately paid her, and it was with honest pride she
mentioned how he had actually lifted her "in his great
strong arms"—to use her own expression—from her
seat beside the kitchen fire to her arm-chair in the
"Sanctum." There is great expression in the tones
of her voice, a musical sweetness which shews a gentle

spirit and a fine ear. Never have we heard the pathetic or the humorous in ballad poetry rendered with such happy effect as in the snatches which she repeated of her own ballads or from the old minstrel lore. She is a *gentlewoman*, in the true sense of that term, by instinct, or by a certain delicacy of feeling, and by self-culture. Her ease, self-possession, native grace, and dignity, all so thoroughly natural and simple—in short, her true *womanliness*—are qualities as remarkable, perhaps, as her poetic genius.

If we may be allowed the expression, she seems to have been a born reader. She can scarcely remember the time when her love of books was not her ruling passion. She had exhausted the village library before she had entered her teens, and the astonished librarian, who had never met with such an instance before, and who had no small pride in his collection of books, was obliged to confess that she had fairly read him out —the Universal History and all; expressing at the same time a fear that she might read herself blind, a fear which has been but too painfully realised. It was very amusing to hear her "ain gudeman," John, telling with great glee, how that after she had "used up" the village library, he went to another at some distance, and brought one armful of books after another,

and continued his journeys till this other librarian was
also compelled to acknowledge that he had never
known a case of such *fell* reading before. It is
noteworthy that the first copies of Milton's Paradise
Lost, and of Allan Ramsay's Poetical Works, which
Janet saw, were on a weaver's loom. Referring to this
treasure, which she found in her eighth year, she very
appropriately quoted the lines from one of her poems,
entitled "A Wheen aul' Memories"—

> "It was there my young fancy first took to the wing;
> It was there I first tasted the Helicon spring;
> It was there wi' the poets I wad revel and dream,
> For Milton an' Ramsay lay on the breast beam."

Being a great reader herself, she was very desirous
that her neighbours in the same walk of life should
share in her pleasure, and so she started a small
circulating library, which, true to poetic experience,
turned out a losing concern. She had no lack of
readers, but they failed to return the volumes they
took out, so that her library was literally exhausted, for
she lost all her books. It was a very praiseworthy
effort, however, which she made for the diffusion of
knowledge.

It was only in connection with one book that any
domestic duty was ever overlooked, or any allotted

task for the day not completed. Her confession on
this subject is memorable. "Shakspeare," she said,
" was my first and only transgression in connection with
my domestic labour, and oh, Sir, need ye wonder at it
when I turned for the first time to his wondrous pages?
I regard him as the first of all poets. I was drawn
to him as if by a special instinct." The case with
which she can quote some of his finest passages is truly
astonishing. He was not only her first poet but her
schoolmaster, for she got her knowledge of grammar,
and her love of poetry at the same time, from the bard
of Avon. On expressing to her our surprise that she
could write so grammatically without having formally
learned any rules, she replied, "Shakspeare was my
teacher; my ear is also a guide so far; and besides all
this, God has given me a good tack (gift) of *nat'ral*
grammar. You might as well ask the laverock how it
can sing as ask me how I can write according to the
rules of grammarians."

When a mere girl, she revelled in the ballad lore of
the country, and drank deeply into its spirit. Her
Grannie had a large collection of old-world stories
and ballads, and these she repeated and sang to the
highly-delighted youngsters who gathered in the winter
evenings around her spinning wheel. Her aged

relative was certainly as remarkable for her retentive memory, and for her large store of floating traditions in song, ballad, and story, as was the old woman who resided in Burns' family.

She quoted, with great enthusiasm, from some old ballads which she believed were written about "the killing time," when the rage of the persecutors blazed out against the Covenanters with the greatest fury. She was of opinion that Hogg had given the essence of some of those ballads in the words which he represents Nanny as singing in the "Brownie of Bodsbeck." The crone herself did not give the lines with such emphasis, and in such a dramatic style, at Chapelhope, as we heard them rendered at Langloan.

The hearty, unrestrained laugh with which Janet closed the vigorous recital of the pithy lines, announcing the doom of "Græme, Lagg, Drumlanrick," and other noted actors in that bloody drama, will long linger in our memory. As a set-off to the scathing fire of that quotation, she gave, with touching pathos, the following verses, which are taken from the same source. They are now printed as they were repeated. If Janet's memory was at fault, her poetic genius was at no loss to supply the defect.

" O, dinna greet, my bonny doo,
    Nor on the present ponder,
    For thou shalt sing on the laverock's wing,
    And far away beyond her.

" When the clouds are high and the well rins dry,
    Then heaven o' earth maun borrow,
    And the mists that stray on the ground to-day
    May sail in heaven to-morrow."

Her love of nature is intense, and, notwithstanding her blindness, the wild flowers are still as near and dear to her as ever. It is remarkable that she has never seen a mountain, nor the sea, nor any river but the Clyde, the Falls of which she has never visited, and she has never been the distance of twenty miles from her humble dwelling. Her region of song, so far as scenery is concerned, has been very limited. It may be all comprised in the glen of the Calder, and the bosky dells and breckan-covered banks of her favourite stream, the Luggie, before it was polluted with the refuse of the furnaces, and its sweet " wilding flowers" covered with slag. That was her fairy rivulet in the days of childhood, and to her youthful imagination it was peopled with everything that was bright, and beautiful, and fair. It was there, when a lassie, she caught the minnows of which she so frequently sings, and gathered in the fairy nooks the primrose, the hyacinth, and the blue bell, her favourite flowers. Again and again, during our brief visit, did she refer with all the warmth of youthful glee to her exploits at "mennin" fishing, which she has described in "Luggie, Past and Present."

It is with all the bitter regret of a genuine poet that she mourns the sad changes which have passed over the streamlet of her childhood. In spite of all these changes, this "burn" and all its sweet memories of life's young day have been to her as a first love. No two streams in Scotland have been more highly honoured than the "Luggie" of David Gray and that of Janet Hamilton.

Her love of the beautiful in nature gleams like a "crystal licht," to use her own expression, through the whole of her three volumes. As a specimen of this, take the following from the "Ballad of Memorie":—

> "Nae mair, alas! nae mair I'll see
>   Young mornin's gowden hair
> Spread owre the lift—the dawnin' sheen
>   O' simmer mornin' fair!
> Nae mair the heathery knowe I'll speel,
>   An' see the sunbeams glancin',
> Like fire-flauchts owre the loch's lane breast,
>   Owre whilk the breeze is dancin'.

> " Nae mair I'll hear the cushie-doo,
>   Wi' voice o' tender wailin',
> Pour out her plaint ; nor laverock's sang,
>   Up 'mang the white clouds sailin' ;
> The lappin' waves that kiss the shore,
>   The music o' the streams,
> The roarin' o' the linn nae mair
>   I'll hear but in my dreams."

The wild primrose happened to be referred to—"Ah! that's my sweet, favourite wilding," she said, and then repeated her own beautiful conception contained in the following lines :—

> "The red-lippit gowan had closed her sweet mou',
>   But the cup o' the primrose was lippin' wi' dew ;
> An' the hy'cinth had kamed oot her ringlets o' blue,
>   Till the dell o' their fragrance an' beauty was fu'."

She concludes one of her recent letters to a friend in these affecting words :—"I must confess feeling a weakness when sitting darkling in my chair, as the woods and fields are pictured in my mind's eye, clothed in their summer garb. All is for the best. James (referring to her son) keeps me pretty well supplied with wilding flowers beloved from childhood."

With her intense love of nature, it will not be surprising to our readers to learn that Shakspeare's description of a bank of wild thyme, in the "Midsummer Night's Dream," has lingered for so many years

D

in her memory, or that it should form one of her
favourite quotations :—

> "I know a bank whereon the wild thyme blows,
> Where ox-lips and the nodding violet grows ;
> Quite over-canopied with lush woodbine,
> With sweet musk-roses, and with eglantine :
> There sleeps Titania."

It was very touching when Mirren, her daughter,
read some of the ballads in this volume, in which
there are beautiful allusions to nature, to hear the
blind old mother say again and again, as she sat bent
forward, eagerly listening, in her arm chair, "I see
it ! I see it a'! It's like a crystal o' licht set in my
very heart." On expressing our surprise that she
could so vividly recall past scenes and speak with
rapture of the wild flowers which she could see no
more, she said, "They're a' in my heart—I loved
them too well ever to forget them ;" and then she
quoted a verse from the "Ballad of Memorie," already
referred to, beginning with the lines—

> "When a' the house are gane to sleep,
> I sit my leefu lane," &c.

Now that we have introduced the daughter Mirren
to our readers, we may add that the aged poetess, during her blindness, has had most kindly help from her

loving hand, and from her "ain aul' guidman," who
regards her with singular devotion. He has been
so much in the practice of reading aloud to her, that
his voice "has got doon," he says, "to a deid hearse-
ness." She has a most affectionate amanuensis in
her son James, who, notwithstanding all his other
duties in connection with his daily work, is ever
delighted to consecrate all his spare hours in writing
to her dictation, "when the burning thochts within,"
as old John expressed it, "winna let her rest."
Mirren is all in all about the house, as the Martha
of the home circle, but she is specially great in
the reading of her mother's ballad poetry. In this
effort her feelings frequently overcame her at any
very touching part of the tale. She was requested
to read the ballad entitled "Effie," which appears
in this volume, and which is perhaps the most
pathetic of all her mother's writings; so she began
in the long-drawn, plaintive cadence suited to the
sad tale, and got on so far; but her voice trembled
and she broke down when she came to the depths of
Effie's sorrows. It was no affectation, but genuine
feeling, which choked her utterance, just as we felt
ourselves when trying to read aloud for the first time
at our own fireside the story of "Rab and his Friends."

Mirren lifted her apron to her face ;—James quietly
left the room ;—old John drew his coat-sleeve across
his eyes ;—there sat the mother, pale and blind, and
bent forward in her chair ; she uttered a word of
encouragement to the reader, but the truth is, we
were all very much in the melting mood.

To relieve the pressure of sad thoughts produced by
the reading of " Effie," Janet asked us if we had ever
tried the writing of *Cento* verses, which she character-
ised as a pleasant literary amusement for a meeting of
young friends in a winter night. On confessing our
ignorance, she forthwith explained the nature of this
effort by giving us a few specimens, which may be
interesting to our readers. The lines and the names
of the authors are now printed as she repeated them.

" Full many a flower is born to blush unseen   *Gray.*
Far in a wild unknown to public view,   *Parnell.*
Beneath a vault unsullied by a cloud,   *Cowper.*
And darkly, deeply, beautifully blue.   *Byron.*

" Long had our pious friend in virtue trode,   *Parnell.*
An honest man's the noblest work of God ;   *Pope.*
Large was his bounty and his soul sincere,   *Gray.*
And passing rich at forty pounds a year.   *Goldsmith.*

" Heaven burns with all its stars,   *Ossian.*
The young May moon is beaming ;   *Moore.*
Thus sang my love, O come with me,   *Campbell.*
The bridal lights are gleaming."   *Cunningham.*

Janet Hamilton is pre-eminently a poet of social progress. This is the thread of gold which runs through all her writings. She feels for the oppressed and suffering everywhere, and she smites, with no sparing hand, and in no measured terms, the vices and the wrongs which have wrought such misery and woe upon the earth. Elizabeth Barrett Browning never penned a more piercing "Cry of the Human," or a more urgent "Cry of the Childern," than Janet has done in some of her own spirit-stirring utterances, born in the depths of her own agony, and wrung from her own bleeding heart by our national curse and disgrace, Intemperance. It is, indeed, a very touching picture to see her seated, pale and blind, in her arm chair, and lamenting, with such anguish of heart, the evils entailed upon the country by this curse. She repeated to us, with trembling emotion, the poem which appears in this volume, entitled "The Enemy still Sits in the Gate."

Humour is another marked characteristic, and her saddest thoughts and utterances were followed by bright flashes of this during our visit.

Her Christian cheerfulness and patient submission in the midst of blindness, and other trials even more severe than this, are, after all, the true poetry of her life, and a pleasant proof to every visitor that a merciful God, who "tempers the wind to the shorn lamb," has given her "songs in the night in this the house of her pilgrimage," and a good hope, through grace, of coming glory, when in the light of God she will see light clearly.

Meantime, dear old friend, in the darkness of life's lengthening shadows which have gathered around thee, a *gloaming* made darker still by the loss of sight, may it be light with thee, and may the " crystal licht" in thy heart never fade, but grow brighter and brighter unto the perfect day!

We cannot close this hasty sketch better than in Janet's own words :—

> " The star o' memory lichts the past ;
> But there's a licht abune,
> To cheer the darkness o' a life
> That maun be endit soon.
> An' aft I think the gowden morn,
> The purple gloamin' fa,'
> Will shine as bricht, and fa' as saft,
> Whan I hae gane awa'."

GLASGOW, *September, 1868.*

POEMS AND BALLADS.

THE SKYLARK—CAGED AND FREE.

SWEET minstrel of the summer dawn,
Bard of the sky, o'er lea and lawn
Thy rapturous anthem, clear and loud,
Rings from the dim and dewy cloud
That swathes the brow of infant morn,
Dame Nature's first and fairest born !
From grassy couch I saw thee spring,
Aside the daisy curtains fling,
Shake the bright dew-drops from thy breast,
Preen thy soft wing, and smooth thy crest—
Then, all the bard within thee burning,
Heaven in thine eye, the dull earth spurning,
Thou soar'dst and sung, till lost on high,
In morning glories of the sky !
   Not warbling at thine own sweet will,
Far up yon " heaven-kissing hill."
With quivering wing, and swelling throat,
On waves of ambient air afloat—
Not so, I saw thee last, sweet bird :

I heard thee, and my heart was stirred,
Above the tumult of a street,
Where smoke and sulphurous gases meet,
Where, night and day, resounds the clamour
Of shrieking steam, of wheel, and hammer—
A Babel rude of many a tongue:
There, high o'erhead, thou blithely sung,
Caged, "cribb'd, confin'd," yet full and clear
As silver lute, fell on my ear
Thy joyous song: as void of sorrow
As when, to bid the sun good morrow,
Just rising from his couch of gold,
Thou sung, and soar'dst o'er mead and wold.
Thy prison song, O bird beloved,
My heart hath strangely, deeply moved.
In reverie, a waking dream
Steals o'er my senses, and I seem
The joyous girl that knew no care,
When fields were green and skies were fair:
And, sweetest of the warbling throng,
The thrilling, gushing, voice of song
I seem to hear.—Ah! 'tis the lark,
That, mounting, "sings at heaven's gate;" hark
These rapturous notes are all his own;
Bard of the sky, he sings alone!
    Sweet captive, though thy fate be mine,
I will not languish—will not pine;
Nor beat my wings against the wires,
In vain regrets and strong desires

To roam again, all blythe and free,
Through Nature's haunts—again to see
The blooming, bright, and beauteous things
That in her train each season brings:
Spring's bursting buds and tender leaves,
The summer flowers, the autumn sheaves,
The purple hills, the shining streams,
Where lingering memory broods and dreams;
But, never more—ah! never more
To climb the hill or tread the shore
With foot untiring, swift, and free—
It may not—nay, it cannot be.
Ah! cannot be! my eyes are dark—
A prisoner, too, like thee, sweet lark:
But I have sought and found content;
And so our songs shall oft be blent—
I, singing in my hermitage,
Thou, warbling in thy prison cage,
Aspire! thou to thine own blue sky,
I to a loftier sphere on high!

OCTOBER.

Not changeful April, with her suns and showers—
Pregnant with buds, whose birth the genial hours
Of teeming May will give to life and light,
Rich in young beauty, odorous, and bright—

Not rose-crowned June, in trailing robes of bloom,
Her flowery censers breathing rich perfume,
Her glorious sunshine and her bluest skies—
Her wealth of dancing leaves where zephyr sighs—

Nor fervid July, in her full-blown charms,
Shedding the odorous hay with sun-browned arms :
Nor glowing August, with her robe unbound,
With ripening grain and juicy fruitage crowned—

Nor thee, September, though thine orchards glow
With fruits ripe, rich, and ruddy—laying low
The yellow grain with gleaming sickle keen,
With jest and laugh, and harvest song between—

I sing OCTOBER—month of all the year
To poets' soul and calm, deep feeling dear.
Her chastened sunshine and her dreamy skies
With tender magic charm my heart and eyes.

In silvery haze the purple hills are swathed,
In dripping dews the faded herbage bathed ;
Red-Robin trills his winter-warning ditty,
His big bright eye invoking crumbs and pity.

From faded woodlands, ever pattering down,
Come many-tinted leaves—red, yellow, brown ;
The rustling carpet, with slow, lingering feet,
I thoughtful tread, inhaling odours sweet.

The very soul of quietude is breathing
O'er field and lake, with sweetest peace enwreathing
My tranquil soul ; from fonts of blissful feeling,
Sweet, silent tears adown my cheek are stealing.

Spirit of meekness—brooding in the air—
On thy soft pinions waft my lowly prayer,
That I may meet—calm, meek, resigned, and sober—
My life's decline—my solemn last October.

MEMORIES.

WRITTEN IN THE STORMY MONTHS OF THE OPENING YEAR, 1868.

LONELY musing, sadly thinking,
Strength and spirits failing, sinking,
Drooping, shivering, cow'ring, shrinking.
   In the wintry blast.
Winds are howling, roaring, screaming,
Thunder rolling, lightning gleaming,
Rain and hail in torrents streaming,
   Driving fierce and fast.

Storms the face of nature marring,
Thunder-clouds conflicting, jarring,
Strife of elemental warring,
   These are calm and tame
To the storms of wrathful feeling,
Human hearts to vengeance stealing,
Wrath of man in deeds revealing
   Rapine, blood, and shame.

Cease, my heart, thy dirge-like knelling!
Why in mournful numbers swelling?
Why my muse thus ever quelling
  Strains of hope and peace?
Change the strain, the flowers are springing?
Hark! the lark at heaven's gate singing!
Ah! his joyous anthem ringing,
  Bids thy wailings cease.

The primrose in the dell is blowing;
Sister flowerets, fresh and glowing,
Grace the brooklet's brink, clear flowing
  Through the dingle green.
To the tassel'd hazel bushes
Now resort the amorous thrushes;
The water coot among the rushes
  Seeks her brood to screen.

Clouds alternate, smiling, weeping,
O'er the April skies are sweeping;
Dancing streams are gaily leaping
  To the pools below.
Thousand small bright eyes are twinkling
Through the leaves, where trilling, tinkling
Song of wild birds gushes, trinkling
  In melodious flow.

In dewy tears the hy'cinth weeping,
Her drooping azure bells is steeping,
The violet's sweet blue eyes are peeping,
    Veiling leaflets through.
With "daisies pied," and cowslips yellow,
Comes the voice that hath no fellow—
Wandering voice, soft, clear, and mellow,
    'Tis the lone cuckoo.

Beauteous spring! with throb and quiver
Beats my heart.   Alas! for ever
My eyes are dark, and I shall never
    See thy smiling face—
Never see the purple heather,
Ne'er the fern's green waving feather,
Never May's sweet blossoms gather,
    On my breast to place.

Be hush'd, my heart! thy 'plaint restraining,
Hush'd be murmuring and complaining,
'Tis the will of God constraining
    Humble resignation.
Bear thy loss without repining,
"Darkest clouds have silver lining,"
On the night of sorrow shining;
    Blessed consolation!

Olden memories never dying,
Treasures in my bosom lying,
The failing founts of life supplying
    With perennial flow.
Memories of the good and holy,
Of the dark and melancholy,
Of the sufferers meek and lowly,
    Sainted long ago.

Memories of the young and loving,
Friendships tried, yet faithful proving,
Scenes to deep compassion moving,
    Cureless, tearless woes.
Memories sweet of rural pleasure,
Streams, and woods, and floral treasure,
Rich the free, unstinted measure
    Nature's hand bestows.

Memory tells of idly dreaming
Life away—of never deeming
That the work of time redeeming
    Being youth begun.
Work! while life's young sun is shining—
Darkness comes, when life, declining,
Weakly, darkly, sadly pining,
    Mourns her work undone.

Memory ever backward flowing,
Of the future all unknowing,
Paints the past in colours glowing,
    This bright memory can.
"The memory of the just is blessed."
Be that bliss by all possessed !
All whose lives are thus expressed,
    "Just to God and man."

ELEGIAC VERSES ON THE DEATH OF LORD PALMERSTON.

A LOFTIER muse, in higher strains, may sing
   A grander requiem o'er the stateman's bier:
Yet genius, rank, and grandeur may not bring
   A holier tribute, or a warmer tear.

"Familiar in our mouths as household words,"
   His name, his talent, and his worth.   Enshrined
In Britain's heart, when memory stirs its chords,
   She boasts the triumphs of his master mind.

The world of politics abroad he scanned
   With eagle glance, that would not quail or pause;
Woe to the despot! whose unholy hand
   Had touched the ark of British rights and laws.

His was no garment rolled in needless blood—
   His voice, no shouting warrior's battle cry;
A Nestor at the council board he stood,
   His counsels ever sage, and purpose high.

E

The demon steed of dark despotic power
    He curbed and reined with might and matchless skill;
When o'er our isle the tempest seemed to lower,
    The brooding clouds were scattered at his will.

" We may not look upon his like again."
    Full oft he passed, avoiding shoal and strand,
O'er diplomacy's deep and treacherous main,
    And brought the good ship Britain safe to land.

Alas! the hand that held the helm is cold—
    The trusted pilot treads the deck no more,
Whose skilful tactics—measures prompt and bold—
    Kept far the dangers of a leeward shore.

His place is vacant at the council board,
    And empty in the senatorial hall;
But in the nation's heart a grateful chord
    Still vibrates strong for him, revered of all.

"WORDS OF COMFORT."

VERSES SUGGESTED BY THE PERUSAL OF A BOOK ENTITLED "WORDS OF
COMFORT," EDITED BY WILLIAM LOGAN, GLASGOW.

"WORDS OF COMFORT," they are come,
 Rich in many a tender token,
Weeping love and mothers' woe,
 Deeply felt and fitly spoken.

"Words of Comfort," ah! to whom
 Do they come? Our Heavenly Father
Comforts all who mourn, bereaved
 Of the flowers His hand doth gather.

"Words of Comfort," rich the balm
 From each precious page distilling,
Softly on the mourner's heart—
 With sweet peace and comfort filling.

"Words of Comfort," on the wings
 Of the morning they are flying,
To the utmost ends of earth,
 Still their bless'd vocation plying.

"Words of Comfort," they have come,
　　To the Mission mother, kneeling
By her infant's timeless grave,
　　Comfort, hope, and heaven revealing.

"Words of Comfort," thus they speak—
　　"Mother, cease to soil with weeping
That pure cheek so cold and pale ;
　　Baby is not dead but sleeping !"

"Words of Comfort," mother, dear,
　　Come to thee, assurance bringing
That the babe thou mourn'st as lost
　　Now before the throne is singing.

"Words of Comfort," bouquet rare !
　　Gemm'd with many an Eden blossom,
Culled with care and placed with love
　　On the mourner's aching bosom.

MARY LEE.

A BALLAD.

WHAT ails ye, bonnie Mary Lee?
    What gars ye greet an' pine?
Your e'e is dim, your cheek is wan—
    What ails ye, Mary, mine?

Kame back, kame back the raven hair
    That wanners owre your broo,
Gae to the burn, lave cheek an' chin,
    My bonnie mournin' doo.

I ken your saunted mither's gane
    The gate we a' maun gae,
But weel we houp she's wi' the blest,
    Then wharfore mourn ye sae?

Come, sit ye doun beside me, lass,
    An' tell your waesume tale—
Sair it maun be, my Mary Lee,
    That mak's yer cheek sae pale.

She drew a creepie to her side,
    An' dichtit aye her een :—
O, Leezie, lass, I'se tell ye a',
    My truest, dearest fiien'.

Ye ken't young Jock o' Benty Knowe,
  A lad that bare the gree,
Whare'er he gaed nae ither Joe
  Was hauf sae dear to me.

For towmonds twa he courtit me;
  At market, kirk, an' fair,
Ye wadna' miss'd him frae my side,
  The brawest, blythest there.

I never thocht to tine his luve,
  Or yet my ain to hide,
An' whan he speer't, I gied consent
  To be his bonnie bride.

Anither towmond we agreed
  To wait; syne fu' an bien
Oor wee cot hoose shou'd plenish't be,
  Baith cozie, tosh, an' clean.

Sune after this, he didna' come
  Sae aften as before;
An' sune nae mair his weel-kenn'd chap
  Cam tirlin' on the door.

An' oh! I thocht my heart wad break!
  I cou'dna think or guess
What I had said or dune to mak'
  Him lo'e me ony less.

An' a' my pride o' maidhood rase !
   I wadna' yield to speer
What had come owre him, tho' I kent
   I lo'ed him true an' dear.

My mournfu' e'e an' wallow't cheek
   My guid aul' faither saw ;
" My bairn," quo' he, " what's come o' Jock !
   He ne'er comes here ava'.

" If he's deceiv'd my bonnie bairn,
   An' cast her luve awa',
Whan he had won her artless heart,
   O ! black sall be his fa' !

" But there's young Jamie o' Blackhill,
   A better man than he,
He lo'es the very yird ye tread,
   My bonnie Mary Lee.

" He's come o' honest godly folk,
   An' leads a sober life,
An' thou hast tauld me that he aft
   Has socht thee for his wife.

" An' but yestreen he said to me,
   If you an' him agree,
Wull you gie me your free guid-wull
   To wed your Mary Lee ?

" An' I ha'e gi'en my free guid-wull,
  An' I sall bless ye baith,
Sae think nae mair o' Benty's Jock,
  He's dune thee scorn an' skaith."

But, Leezie, Jamie o' Blackhill
  Was never nocht to me,
Tho' ne'er a nae-say he wad tak',
  Or ever let me be.

Ae nicht, whan stan'in at the door,
  I saw him comin' roun'
The gavel-en'; an' oh, my heart
  Gied sic a waesume stoun!

Sae blythe and bauld he stappit up,
  "Noo, Mary," whisper'd he,
" I'm come to seek ye for my ain,
  Your faither's pleased wi' me.

" Let byganes a' be byganes noo,
  An' say ye'll be my wife,
Ye'll ne'er hae cause to rue the word
  Your langest day in life."

My faither then cam' to the door,
  An' brocht him kin'ly ben,
Syne bade me bring the bread an' cheese,
  An' fill the tappit hen.*

          * Old pewter pint measure.

An' lang an' couthie was the crack,
    But ne'er a word said I,
Till faither said—Hech, Mary, lass,
    Ye'r unco dull and shy.

Neist owk, my lass we'll buy the braws,
    To busk oor bonnie bride,
For sune ye to the kirk maun gang,
    Wi' Jamie by yer side.

For I've been tauld what to my bairn
    I like na weel to tell,
That Benty Knowe has a' the while
    Been coortin' Bartie's Bell.

I've seen o' simmers aughty-seven,
    An' sune maun lea' thee, bairn,
An' had it been wi' Benty's Jock,
    Thou wad been sair forfairn.

But Jamie is a truthfu' chiel,
    An' lo'es thee as his life,
An' fain am I afore I dee,
    To see thee made his wife.

Wi' thy consent, on Sabbath neist,
    He'll juist pit in the cries;
An' Beuty Knowe an' mony mae
    Will get a great surprise.

O, Leezie, lass, what wad ye dune
   Had ye been in my place?
That nicht I kneel't afore the Lord
   An' pray'd for help o' grace—

That I micht schule my rebel heart
   To dae my faither's will;
For oh! hoo sall I tell thee, lass,
   I lo'e the fautor still.

Neist Sabbath we were cried in kirk;
   On Monday nicht cam' he;
His face was white as ony ghaist,
   The tear was in his e'e.

I maist had swarf't whan to the door
   I gaed and saw him staun,
He cou'dna leuk me in the face,
   But tried to tak' my haun.

But I drew back :—" What want ye, Jock?
   Hae ye come here to tell
Hoo in your wooin' you hae sped
   Wi' Bartie's bonny Bell?

" Ye've dune yer best to break my hert,
   An' smoor't wi' grief an' shame
But if ye can forgie yersell,
   I'se try to dae the same."

He leukit up, an' sic a leuk,
    Sae fu' o' shame an' wae!—
That leuk I never sall forget
    Until my deein' day.

I turn'd me richt an' roun' aboot,
    " Fareweel, fareweel for life !"
Said I: " Whan neist ye see me, Jock.
    I'm Jamie Wilson's wife."

My faither by the crusie sat,
    The Bible on his knee ;
I flung my airms aroun' his neck—
    " O, faither, pray for me !"

He drew me doun upon his knee,
    An' dichtet aff my cheek
The het, het tears ; my heart was fu',
    He saw I cou'dna' speak.

" Oh, I hae pray'd, an' I sall pray
    For thee baith e'en an' morn ;
A dearer or a better bairn
    Was ne'er o' woman born."

An' noo I'll murne an' pine nae mair,
    But tent my faither's life
Wi' muckle care, an' strive to be
    Kin' Jamie's faithfu' wife.

BARNSLEY COLLIERY EXPLOSION.

LINES SUGGESTED BY HEARING OF THE RECENT DREADFUL COLLIERY EXPLOSIONS, WITH THE ATTENDANT FEARFUL LOSS OF LIFE AT THAT PLACE, 1866.

FAR, far below, oh, far below,
Where sulphurous lightnings flash and glow,
Where blasting, bellowing thunders roar
With rending crash—dark Stygian shore ;
Black gulf of horrors, dark, profound,
Where ambush'd demons lurk around—
Waiting to light the horrid gloom
With lurid, scorching, fiery spume
Of deadly gases.   Woe, oh woe !
How long, how long shall it be so ?
How long be sacrificed in vain
These hideous hecatombs of slain ?
Pale Science weeps, her troubled eye
Falls on the victims as they lie—
Scorched, crushed, and mutilated forms,
Dire wrecks of subterranean storms,
That ravage with resistless sweep
Those regions of the deeper deep.
For she had studied, searched, and toiled,
Had seen her best inventions foiled
With " can't be troubled," "'tis no use,"

"Too much expense," neglect, abuse
Of her injunctions.   Hark! the shock
Explosive through the cavern rock,
The scathing fire, the choking damp.
"Do you not use the safety lamp?"
You ask of some poor writhing wretch.
"The fireman quite forgot to fetch
The warning light.   Alas, alas!
Our naked lights fired off the gas;
The mine was foul, and must explode,
And then along the flame-swept road
A hundred smouldering corpses lay.
Yet I survive—woe worth the day!"
What wailing shrieks, what groans of woe,
What tears of burning anguish flow
From eyes that weep the heart-springs dry!
What *calls* that meet with no reply!
The grey-haired widow calls her boy—
Her duteous lad, her pride and joy;
Sobbing, the newly wedded wife
Calls on the partner of her life;
The widowed mother to her breast
Her orphan babe hath closely pressed;
And, followed by a childish train,
Calls on the father's name in vain.
Alas! that voice, once loved and dear,
Will reach no more his death-closed ear.
Now angel Pity, hand in hand
With Charity, walks through the land;

Benevolence, strong in wealth and power,
Sheds from both hands a golden shower,
Till hearts bereaved hail, even in grief,
With grateful tears the blest relief.
Ah ! it is well it should be so :
But there are words of deeper woe
" Than even the wail above the dead."
What of the soul so quickly sped
To that dark bourne, that unknown shore
Whence traveller can return no more ?
We may not lift the awful veil,
Nor, if we might, would it avail ;
Their state is fixed ; yet all must know
Who labour in the " shades below,"
That, standing face to face with death,
He with a blast—a flash—a breath
May quench the life.   Then oh, beware !
You may with caution, means, and care,
And trust in Providence Divine,
Avert the dangers of the mine.

OCTOBER, 1865.

As by the deathbed of an aged saint,
Whose pallid lips emit no moaning plaint,
On whose calm brow the light of heaven is shed,
Eternal peace begun ere life has fled—
Even so I stand and gaze with moistened eyes
On the calm glories of the autumn skies,
The breathless quiet, "the rapture of repose"
That o'er the dying form of Nature throws
A magic halo, a soul-trancing spell,
A powerful charm to soothe, perchance dispel
The low'ring clouds of care.—I walk abroad,
And, musing, stray along the silent road,
Or by the margin of the moaning stream,
Whose mournful music aids the poet's dream—
A dream of bliss and peace, serene and sober—
The dream, the bliss, the peace are thine, October:
Thine the sear leafage of the rifled woods,
The fading hue of pastoral solitudes;
Thy groves are silent—there the cushat-dove
No more in amorous cooings tells her love,
And save red-robin of the noisless wing,
And short, shrill lay, we hear no warbler sing;
Beneath the beech the mast lies ripe and brown,
The ripen'd acorns patter thickly down.

Fast in their jagged husks the chestnuts fall;
Far in the hazel copse I hear the call
Of merry nutters beating down the spoil,
Their kernel treasures, meed of pleasant toil.
Where now the flowers decayed, discoloured, dead?
Still here and there the daisy rears her head,
All blanched and tearful, as if sadly weeping
The death of kindred in the dank sod sleeping.
Oh close thy weary lids, dim " Eye of day,"
Till spring shall wake and raise thee from the clay;
For thou shalt wake again, again shall rise
To gaze again upon the summer skies,
To drink the dew, and feel the brushing wing
Of early lark, ere yet he mounts to sing.
And I, like thee, lone floweret, must decay—
Must soon be laid to sleep with kindred clay,
Till time shall be no more, and earth and sky,
With all they hold, in flaming ruins lie ;
Then death itself shall die, and earth restore
Her sleepers in the dust—to die no more.

SHEEPIEKNOWE.

A Ballad.

Aul' Sheepieknowe! how dear the name!
  Lane birthplace o' my gude forbears :
Scene o' their life-lang cares an' toils,
  Their sunny joys an' cloudy fears.

O! mony a simmer sun has shone,
  An' mony a wintry blast has blawn
On thy laigh heather-theekit roof,
  An' aul' grey wa's that steively staun.

An' mony a bairn first saw the licht
  Aneath thy sooty, strang roof-tree—
That leev'd an' lov'd, an' toil'd, an there
  Lay doun in faith an' hope to dee.

An' mony a bonnie lass, I ween,
  Wi' blushin' cheek an' dooncast e'e,
In bridal gear thy cozie biel
  Has left a dautit wife to be.

An' aft frae oot thy lowly door
  The dead, wi' reverend hauns, were ta'en
To aul' Cam'nethan's lane kirkyard,
  To sleep wi' frien's lang ages gane.

F

An' ilka nicht an' morn were heard
   The soun' o' psalms, the voice o' prayer,
By faither raised, an' sweetly joined
   By wife an' bairnies roun' him there.

Hoo welcome was the Sabbath rest !
   Hoo sweet the Sabbath's holy calm !
On toilin' haun an' weary heart
   It fell like heaven's ain blessed balm.

(May Scotlan' never quat the grip,
   But haud her Sabbath firm an' fast,
Thro' skaith an' scorn, thro' taunts an' sneers.
   An' let them lauch wha win at last.)

Thro' thy wee winnocks, Sheepieknowe,
   Fell little sunshine in the cot ;
Withoot, the beekin' simmer sun
   Lay shadowless upon the spot.

The purple scad o' heather blooms
   Fell on the e'e for acres roun';
But peesweep's cry and muirfowl's ca'
   Ye wadna heard anither soun.'

A gowany sheet lay on the lee,
   Spread by the hauns o' bonnie June ;
Ilk simmer morn, on flichterin' wing,
   The laverock liltit hie abune.

The wuds o' Murdiestane were green,
  An' ringin' wi' the sang-birds' lay;
On Calder's wild an' wannerin' stream
  The glintin' sunbeams saftly play.

In dowie mood, ae simmer day,
  Alang the bank an' up the dell,
I wanner'd on.   There's something wrang.
  I said, but what I canna tell.

A shadow lay upon my heart,
  The feydom o' some comin' ill;
I heard a stap, an' leukin' up,
  Saw Cousin Hughie o' the Hill.

White as a ghaist, wi' bluidshot een,
  He grasp'd an' chirted sair my haun;
"Oh Hughie!" then I gaspit oot,
  "I thocht ye in a foreign lan'."

"To me a' lan's are foreign noo—
  Nae hame, nae haud ha'e I on yirth;
In burnin' shame, an' bitter wae,
  I curse the hour that gied me birth.

"For she, wha's name I canna speak,
  The woman that was ance my wife,
Has brocht disgrace upon my name,
  An blastit a' my hopes in life.

" Ae year, nae mair, in luve an' bliss,
  I spent wi' her, whan we were wed,
But luve, an' bliss, an' purity,
  An' a' the wife should ha'e, have fled.

" I boud to leeve an' gang aboard
  As surgeon in a man-o'-war ;
Twa years frae hame, yet a' the while
  She was my idol an' my star.

" We cam' to port, an' I got leeve,
  An' flew on wings o' luve to rush
Into her arms, an' in my face
  She leukit up withoot a blush.

" Her crime, like murder, wadna hide ;
  My frien's had kenn'd ere I cam' hame,
But had nae heart to sen' me word,
  Sae bauld was she, e'en in her shame.

" I'll never leuk on her again,
  Nor 'gainst my life will raise my haun ;
Neist owk I sail to seek for death
  By Afric's fever-stricken stran'.

" An' I am here ance mair to see—
  Ance mair to tread upon the heather—
The wuds an braes o' Murdiestane,
  Before I lea' them a' thegither."

Like ane entranced I stude the while,
  The tears were streaming down my cheek ;
"God help, and guide thee, cousin dear"—·
  Anither word I cou'dna speak.

He took my haun again, an' said,
  "Fareweel for ever, I maun gae."—
I never saw his face again,
  But mourn'd him sair for mony a day.

But, ere the heather bloomed again,
  An' ere the gowans clad the lea,
He slept intil a foreign grave :
  Rest, weary heart !—peace, peace to thee !

GIRLISH REMINISCENCES.

CRADLED in a nest of flowers,
Sheltered by the birchen bowers
   That clustered round the spot,
Waving their pensile, slender arms,
Shedding a thousand fragrant charms
   Around our lowly cot.

How oft in balmy breathing June,
When woodland choirs were full in tune,
   I wandered by the stream
That poured, in gushing liquid tones,
Its silvery music o'er the stones:
   O happy, happy dream!

And see, while peals of laughter wild
Ring through the wood, a happy child
   Comes plashing down the stream;
Another, and another see—
Four girlish butterflies were we—
   Sporting in life's young dream.

Too soon awake, alas! we found
That it was but enchanted ground
  On which we danced along,
With flowing hair and bounding feet,
With frolic, glee, and laughter sweet,
  And childhood's careless song.

Dear Agnes, very fair and pale
Was she.   How shall I tell the tale?
  Within a lonesome place
They found her lifeless on the ground,
Near where a woodland streamlet wound,
  That rippled o'er her face.

Sweet Mary, with the ringlets fair,
And Helen of the raven hair,
  Where now—oh! where are ye?
Ye crossed the wild Atlantic wave;
Yet still to know, my heart would crave,
  If ye remember me.

And I, I wait upon the shore,
That whoso leaves returns no more;
  I long to reach my Home,
Where those not lost, but gone before,
Shall meet on that celestial shore
  Where death nor sorrows come.

A LAY OF THE LOCH AN' THE MUIRLAN'.

"THE SHORT AND SIMPLE ANNALS OF THE POOR."

A LANELY loch, a muirlan' broon,
　A warl' o' whins an' heather,
Whaur aft, whan life was young, I strayed,
　The berries blae to gather.
Sae bonnie bloomed the gowden broom,
　Sae green the feathery bracken,
An' rosy brier, dear to my e'en,
　Ere licht had them forsaken.

Hoo saftly, calmly, sweetly fell
　That dewy, simmer gloamin',
Whan I alang the lanely loch
　To muse and dream gaed roamin'.
The star o' luve her lamp had lit,
　The sun's last rays were glancin'
Oot owre the wee, wee curlin' waves,
　Like water-spunkies dancin'.

The wild duck stay'd her paidlin' feet
    To nestle 'mang the rashes,
The loupin' braise an' perch fell back
    Wi' mony plouts an' plashes ;
An' there, deep anchored in the loch,
    The water lilies floatin',
Like pearly skiffs to bear the crews
    Whan fairies tak' to boatin'.

O ! is't a maiden's mournfu' sang
    That owre the loch is stealin',
In strains sae waesome an' sae sweet,
    A tale o' luve revealin' ?
If sae, she sings nae a' her lane :
    Hark ! frae that lanely dwallin'
Sweet voices mair than twa or three
    The silvery chorus swallin'.

O ! leeze me on that laigh wee cot,
    The hame o' Wabster Johnnie ;
An' leeze me on his dochters five,
    A' warkrife, gude, an' bonny.
An' oh ! hoo sweet at gloamin' hour
    To hear thae lassies singin',
An' " Banks an' braes o' bonnie Doon "
    Alang the waters ringin'.

Noo Johnnie was a wabster gude,
   An honest man an' truthfu';
Tho' saxty winters snaw'd his pow,
   He leukit hale an' youthfu'.
Gude hame-spun yarn he weel could weave,
   In druggit, harn, or blanket,
For cotton yarn, the feckless trash,
   Nae customer he thankit.

O! weel he lo'ed his gude auld wife,
   A canty, clever body,
That wrocht her wark, an' ca'd her pirns,
   An' never needed toddy.
An' peace was in their lowly hame,
   They lo'ed ilk ither truly;
An' love an' peace will often meet,
   Whaur God is worshipp'd duly.

An' wooers aften cam' galore
   To see thae lassies bonnie—
A' decent chiels—for unco strict
   Anent his bairns was Johnnie.
An' wad ye ken what them befel
   Whan frae the wabster's ingle
The fivesum gaed to ither hames
   Wi' unco folk to mingle?

First bonnie Jean, syne couthie Jen',
 An' blithesome, winsome Annie,
Were wed, an' passed wi' kind gudemen
 Alang life's road fu' canny.
But Mysie, aye sae blate an' douce,
 An' Nannie snell an' clever,
Baith kept their hauns to ser' themsel's
 In single life for ever.

An' toddlin' wee things cam' belyve
 To see their lochside grannie—
To climb the knees, an' clasp the necks
 O' Aunties May an' Nannie.
An' time an' tide, that bide for nane,
 Brocht changes grit an' mony,
An' scored the broo, an' dimm'd the een,
 An' boo'd the back o' Johnnie.

The treddles noo cam' to a staun,
 The lay nae mair gaed duntin',
An' by the fire he maistly sat,
 His cutty seldom luntin'.
The sisters saw wi' tearfu' een
 That grannie's health was failin',
An' tended her wi' muckle care,
 For she was sairly ailin'.

The twa, sae pleasant in their lives,
  In death were undivided—
Ae heart, ae hope on yirth, ae hame
  In Heaven by grace provided.
Three owks between the sair-worn clay,
  To mither yirth's safe keepin'
Were gi'en. Lang ha'e the aged pair
  Been in her bosom sleepin'.

The loch is lanely noo nae mair;
  Whaur heather, broom, an' bracken
Ance clad the muir, the yellow corn
  By wastlin' win's is shaken;
An' Johnnie's cot the iron hoof
  O' railroad desecration
Has trampit doun—see, there's the line,
  An' there's the railway station.

VERSES

WRITTEN FOR, AND INSCRIBED TO, THE MEMBERS OF THE GLASGOW SAINT ANDREW'S SOCIETY, AT THEIR ANNUAL MEETING, NOVEMBER 30, 1866.

HAIL, Brothers! true sons of the mother we love,
Fair Scotland, free Scotland! we meet here to prove
The filial devotion, that warms as it fills
Our hearts for the Queen of the Lakes and the Hills.

With our hearts, with our hands, our blood and our
    breath,
The fealty we owe her in life and in death
Shall be paid at the altar of Freedom divine,
And the record inscribed on her holiest shrine.

Great WALLACE we honour, the first on the scroll
Of patriots immortal, the godlike in soul :
Strength, valour and glory, unsullied and bright,
Thrice saving his country from tyranny's might.

Ye Sons of ST. ANDREW! sworn brothers in heart,
You have nobly sustained the true patriot's part ;
For Wallace and Scotland ye boldly stood forth,
Till success had crowned the Rock Gem of the North.

No region, no distance, no kingdom or clime,
Can sever the sympathies, high and sublime,
That the sons of old Scotland have felt and expressed
For brethren in bondage, by tyrants oppressed.

In our hearts, GARIBALDI ! thy place hath been given
Near Liberty's martyr, our WALLACE, in Heaven :
Like valour, like virtues, unselfish and pure ;
Thou conquer'd, hast suffer'd, hast learned to endure.

Thou, KOSSUTH, wert priest at fair Liberty's shrine,
When the Hapsburg had mingled her blood with the
      wine ;
But the bloody libation was poured not in vain,
The priest at her shrine shall be KOSSUTH again.

Reformers, we urge not the tide of Reform
With the shock of the earthquake, the roar of the storm,
Advancing, progressive, majestic and grand,
Till sweeping resistless, it rolls o'er the land.

This night in the shade of the Thistle we meet,
As Scotsmen, as freemen, our brothers to greet.
Long may the proud emblem triumphantly wa.e,
The boast of the free, and the hope of the slave.

GARIBALDI'S MISSION.

Garibaldi! Garibaldi!
  Bleeds and burns my heart for thee!
Freedom! union for Italia!
  Never can be won by thee.

Dipp'd in freedom's sacred fountain,
  Waved on high his conquering brand;
Onward now, we strike for Venice!
  Follow me each patriot band.

Kingcraft, Statecraft—Garibaldi!
  Diplomacy, deep and dark,
Rules the hour; 'twere better never
  To have left thy island ark.

Ah! thou high heroic spirit!
  Soul of honour, heart of truth!
Wounded eagle of the Tyrol!
  Take these tears of love and truth.

" What dost thou hear?" O! Garibaldi,
  Place and service are not thine—
Thine to serve the King Eternal
  In a warfare more divine.

Thine to bear high Heaven's commission,
   Thine to wield the Spirit's sword;
Soldier of the Cross, a victor
   In the battles of the Lord.

Not with shouting of the warrior,
   Not with garments rolled in blood,
Canst thou conquer for Italia's
   Truest, highest, lasting good !

LEDDY MARY—A BALLAD.

O! MIRK was the nicht, an' the hour it was late,
Whan a bonnie young leddy gaed up the gate;
Sae slow was her stap—sae sair was the mane
That fell frae her lips aye noo an' again.
She was row'd in a mantle baith rich an' wide,
But page nor maiden were there by her side.
She stude at a door, an' she tirl'd the sneck;
An aul' wife cam' but, wi' a boo an' a beck;
She thocht the rich mantle, an' white-jewel'd haun,
Belang'd to some leddy o' rank in the lan'.
"O! ha'e ye a room ye can put me intil?
Can ye gi'e me a bed, an' gi'e me yer skill?
For here I maun bide till my bairnie is born—
For I maun be deid, or hame on the morn,
An' ye s'all ha'e gowd, an' bountith, an' fee;
But whaur I ha'e come frae, or what I may be,
Ye never maun speer; for nae livin' on yirth
Maun ken what I'm here for, my name, or my birth."
She gie'd her a room, an' she gied her a bed;
She gied her her skill.   Whan twa hours were sped,
The lady was lichter—but she cou'dna bruck
On the face o' her wee greetin' laddie to leuk:
"My heart it wad saften, an' that maunna be
Till I ha'e revenge on his faither," said she.

O ! rich were the pearlin's, an' costly the lace,
That lay on the bosom, and roun' the sweet face
That was droukit wi' tears like a lily wi' dew,
An' her e'e it was stern, tho' her words were few.
She drew frae her bosom a lang purse o' gowd—
"Tak' that for propine, fu' weel it's bestow'd ;
Ye did what ye cou'd for helpin' o' me ;
Twa hours an nae mair I'll tarry wi' thee."
An' true to the time she gat up on her feet,
An' said—"Noo, ye maunna leuk oot on the street;
My gate I maun gang, my weird I maun dree,
In my faither's at hame this day I maun be."
An' sae she gaed oot as she cam' in the dark,
But to whaur she wad gang the wife had nae mark.
She tended the bairn, an' warm'd his wee feet,
Laid him intil the bed, an' sat doun to greet ;
She fear'd the sweet leddy wad come by her deid,
An' naebody near her that kenn'd o' her need.
Neist day thro' the city word gaed like a bell,
That a nobleman's dochter had deet by hersel' ;
On the flure o' her room she was lying cauld deid,
Her mantle rowt roun' her, the hood on her heid.
Whan the wife heard the news it stoun'd her oot thro':
My sweet Lady Mary ! my bonnie young doo !
It maun ha'e been thee that was wi' me yestreen ;
In the pride o' thy beauty hoo aft I ha'e seen
Thee trippin' the street on thy gay gallant's arm !
My malison on him that wrocht thee sic harm !

THE MUSIC OF THE STREAM.

Is it a spirit voice—an angel's song—
That pours its liquid melody among
The mossy stones that break the rippling sheen,
Lone Calder! gliding thy fair banks between?

No! 'tis the voice—the music of the stream,
That chimes harmonious with the poet's dream :
A dream of beauty, radiant and divine,
A halo floating round the muses' shrine.

Oft in sweet summer prime I singing strayed
Down yon deep dell and through the woodland glade,
To woo fair Nature in soft Doric rhymes,
And hear the tinkling of thy silver chimes.

And, ah, what glorious wealth of wilding flowers!
What wealth of fragrant blossoms on thy bowers!
What odorous breathings of the summer breeze !
What chorus of sweet singers in the trees !

O Nature ! fairer, dearer to my heart
Than pictured scenes of highest, rarest art !
What sweeter chord can charm the spirit dream
Than the weird music of the singing stream ?

Fond Memory treasures in her deepest cell
The woodland glade, the deep romantic dell,
Where oft the summer day too brief would seem,
When wandering, musing, by lone Calder's stream.

"A change came o'er the spirit of my dream,"
I heard no more the music of the stream:
The flowers and blooms were withered, trampled, soiled,
Nature's fair face of every charm despoiled.

For, lo! obscuring the fair light of day,
The genii of the mines, in grim array,
With baleful wings the landscape shadowed o'er,
And beauty, bloom, and song exist no more.

OCTOBER MUSINGS, 1866.

SILENT, grave, subdued, and sober,
Month beloved, my own October!
Resting in thy peaceful arms,
Seeing not, I feel thy charms—
Feel upon my withered cheek
Thy gentle breath, thy whispers meek ;
Tell of Autumn's latest sheaves,
Songless woods, and falling leaves—
Nature's floral wreath despoiled ;
Hueless, scentless, matted, soiled,
Fall her tresses thin and gray,
Bending to October's sway.

   Summer sun with thirsty beams
Drinking dry the pools and streams :
Where thy fervid glories now,
The burning splendours of thy brow ?
Veiled effulgence now is thine,
Tender radiance, half divine ;
This dreamy quiet, this stilly calm,
Sheds around a soothing balm.
Hushed beneath the influence mild,
My soul is like a weanèd child—
Weaned from earth's low cares and joys,
Vain pursuits, and worthless toys.

Life's short race is nearly run,
And the goal will soon be won ;
Still I bear in heart and mind
The wants and sufferings of my kind.
   Sad, yet sweet, to moralise
'Neath October's solemn skies,
When the finger of decay
Points the year's declining day ;
Like the hand upon the wall,
" Born to die," inscribes on all :
Flowers decayed and earth defiled,
Where of late they bloomed and smiled ;
Fields and wood's dim, bare, and gray,
In every aspect of decay,
Tell me that I too must die—
In cold decay and darkness lie,
Till He, whose name I love and trust,
Shall wake to life my sleeping dust.

THE BALLAD O' MARY MUIREN.

THE pride o' the clachan, the rose o' the glen,
The flower o' oor lasses was Mary Muiren ;
Sae modest, an' mensefu', an' winsome was she,
Sae couthie, an' blithesome, an' bonnie to see.

What wooers ha'e said, an' what poets ha'e sung,
'Bout bonnie Scotch lassies, sweet, lo'esome, an' young,
I needna repeat ; sae I winna say mair,
But Mary was gentle, an' guileless, an' fair.

In a howe o' the muirlan'—they ca'd it the glen—
Stude a laigh-theekit hoose, wi' a but an' a ben,*
An' gushin', an' rowin', an' wimplin' alang,
A clear, siller burnie was singin' its sang.

In the glen the young gowan first open'd her e'e,
The bluebell an' primrose there first ye micht see ;
The bracken was greenest, the sweet heather bell
The reddest and richest that bloom'd on the fell.

Ae sweet simmer mornin' I gaed awa' doun
Thro' the glen, by the burn—I was gaun to the toun :
Sic a scene o' saft beauty ne'er fell to my e'en,
Sae dewy an' fragrant, sae flowery an' green.

* The country parlour and kitchen.

Hoo saftly fell doon on my warl'-weary breast,
The beauty, the loneliness, silence, and rest
O' the glen, whaur nae soun' ye wad hear at ilk turn
But the sang o' the birdies, an' babblin' burn.

The gate I was gaun brocht me to the hoose-en',
The dwallin' o' Mary, the rose o' the glen.
Her faither—Aul' John—was the canny bit laird
O' the laigh-theekit hoose an' muckle kail-yard.

The hoose fire was luntin, I ken'd by the smeek
Rowin' oot o' the lum, an' the guff o' peat reek
I snufft wi' delight : sae the folk were asteer,
An' I thocht in the by-gaun for them I wad speer.

There was nae lockit yett, an' nae bow-wowin' tyke
To keep me frae stappin' inside o' the dyke ;
It was juist when Aul' Johnnie was raisin' the saum—
The beuk it was ta'en in the quiet mornin' caum.

That voice it was naebody's, Mary, but thine,
The highest, the sweetest, the hauflins divine ;
It rang in my lug like a clear siller bell,
An' my heart hoo it dinil't aneath the sweet spell.

The door it was open'd, an' Mary cam' oot,
As sweet as a rose an' as fresh as a trout.
She smiled when she saw me, an' bade me gae in ;
It was time for the milkin', sae aff she bound rin.

There was naebody there as I stappit in ben,
But John an' his wife sittin' on the fire-en'.
" Your welcome," quo' he, an' the licht on his face
Was the spirit o' peace an' caum prayerfu' grace.

The wife leukit up, an' I saw by her e'e
That her heart was as dowie as dowie micht be ;
I thocht that some grief maun ha'e lain on it lang ;
Wi' Mary, sweet Mary, sure nocht cou'd be wrang.

" O Nannie, it's weel ye ha'e come to the glen,
I ha'e something to speer that ye aiblins may ken.
O, I ha'e been dwinin' this towmond an' mair,
Gey doun i' the mouth, an' a heart fu' o' care.

Amang your acquaintance doun by in the toun,
Ken ye ocht o' a chiel whase name is Tam Broon ?
He's a braw, swankie fallow as ever ye saw,
An' a tongue that wad wile e'en the egg frae the craw.

Three nichts i' the owk he comes doun to the glen,
An' aftener, maybe, for ocht that I ken ;
He's a'thing wi' Mary, that's plain to be seen,
An' he's juist drawn the heuks owre my puir lassie's een.

Some freen's they ha'e tauld us he's aften seen fu',
An' atweel I jalouse that the tale is owre true ;
But Mary, she says it's a' lees that they tell,
For Tam is the man can tak' care o' himsel'.

Her faither forbids her to speak to the man,
An' I greet, an' I pray, an' say what I can.
'O mither,' she says, 'I ha'e gi'en him my heart,
An' my haun he maun ha'e, for the twa canna part.'"

"Weel, neebor, for you an' puir Mary I'm wae,
That a chiel like Tam Broon shou'd ha'e tack'lt ye sae;
I ken him fu' weel, an' he's gi'en to the dram,
But sleekit, an' pawkie, and guid at a sham."

Alas! for puir Mary, sae sweet, an' sae fair,
She teuk nae advice. sae they priggit nae mair:
Ere lang she was wedded tae sleekie Tam Broon,
Nor lang till she faund him a fause, drucken loon.

Three towmonds an' mair I was far frae the glen,
An' ne'er cou'd hear tell o' puir Mary Muiren,
But whan I cam' back to my hame in the toun,
To speer for the bodies I gaed awa' doun.

Whan I stappit in by, no ane cou'd I see
But John by the fire, wi' a bairn at his knee—
A bonnie wee lassie, wi' lang gowden hair,
The image o' Mary, but she wasna there.

He rose when he saw me, an' grippit my haun;
His een were watshod, an' he cou'dna weel staun.
"O Nannie, my woman, sin' ye gaed awa',
My sorrows and losses they hinna been sma'.

It's a towmond come June sin' I lost my auld wife,
An' wi' her a' the comfort an' hope o' my life ;
Wi' grief her grey hairs to the grave were brocht doon,
An' wha had the wyte o't but drucken Tam Broon.

An' syne my puir Mary, his heart-stricken wife,
Wha ance was the pleasure an' licht o' my life,
Sax months sin', wi' sorrow an' poortith oppressed,
Was laid on her mither's cauld bosom to rest.

I thought then to dee, but the Lord he has lent
This sweet bairn to me wi' her faither's consent ;
An' my Mary's wee Mary is mine noo to keep,
To eat o' my bread, in my bosom to sleep."

"Frien' Johnnie," said I, as I dichtit my een,
"This bairn for a blessin' to you may be gi'en :
May the hap o' her mither ne'er darken her life,
May she ne'er dree the dule o' the drucken man's wife."

THE SUNDAY RAIL—I.

On the Opening of the North British Railway for running
Sunday Trains, September 3, 1865.

Now range up the carriages, feed up the fires!
To the rail, to the rail, now the pent up desires
Of the pale toiling million find gracious reply.
On the pinions of steam they shall fly, they shall fly,
The beauties of nature and art to explore,
To ramble the woodlands and roam by the shore.
The city spark here with his smart smirking lass,
All peg-topp'd and crinolined, squat on the grass:
While with quips and with cranks, and soft-wreathed
    smiles,
Each nymph with her swain the dull Sabbath beguiles.
Here mater and pater familias will come
With their rollicking brood from their close city home.
How they scramble and scream, how they scamper and
    run,
While pa and mamma are enjoying the fun !
And the urchins bawl out, " Oh how funny and jolly,
Dear ma, it is thus to keep Sabbath-day holy !"
Now for pipe and cigar, and the snug pocket flask,
What's the rail on a Sunday without them, we ask ?
What the sweet-scented heather and rich clover blooms
To the breath of the weed as it smoulders and fumes?

So in courting and sporting, in drinking and smoking,
Walking and talking, in laughter and joking,
They while the dull hours of the Sabbath away.
What a Sabbath it is!   Who is lord of the day?
Son of man, Son of God, in the sacred record,
'Tis written that thou art of Sabbath the Lord;
But impious man hath reversed the decree,
And declares himself lord of the Sabbath to be.

In a world without souls it might not be amiss
The Sabbath to spend in such fashion as this;
But men having souls, if aware of the fact,
Should remember the Sabbath to keep it intact.
For souls are immortal, and bodies are clay,
And life but a vapour that fleeteth away;
To the soul and to God in His worship be given,
Oh, is it too much?—'tis but one day in seven.

THE SUNDAY RAIL.—II.

A Scottish Summer Sabbath Morning.

THE still repose, the holy calm
Of this blest morn, a sacred balm
Sheds on my world-worn weary heart;
Its quiet beatitudes impart
A peace benign, a yearning love,
A wish for perfect peace above.
  The liquid music of the rill;
The crow of muircock on the hill;
The chirping, twittering, warbling gush
Of feathered throats in brake and bush;
And high o'erhead, on quivering wings,
The lark her thrilling anthem sings.
These only are the sounds I hear;
But ah! I feel that God is near—
Near to the soul that from her wings
Shakes off the soil of earthly things
That mar her flight and chill her life
Through six days' care, and toil, and strife.
Thank God, to us one day in seven,
The blessed Sabbath rest is given—
Given that the soul may prune her wing,
And to the Sabbath altar bring;

And on its sacred circle lay
The hallowed offerings of the day,—
Thoughts, winged with faith, that to the skies
In prayer and meditation rise.

　To praise Thy name and hear Thy Word,
Within Thy sacred temple, Lord,
Our love and duty we unite,
And call the Sabbath a delight.
Not such the Sunday tourist feels
When on the steam-car's rushing wheels,
In quest of health and recreation—
We add, of pleasure and flirtation—
He flies along the sounding line
And thinks the day indeed divine;
And says, "From bigot trammels free,
The Sunday holiday for me!"
Oh, Scottish workmen! Oh, my brothers!
I plead with you above all others:
Why lose your prestige?—why backslide
From fathers, once their country's pride,
From whom you boast you are descended?
Ah, they could ne'er have apprehended
That ye, their sons by blood and name,
Should thus dishonour—shame! oh, shame!—
The Hallowed Day, ordained most holy,
By idle pleasure, sin and folly.

BALLAD OF THE MONKLAND COTTAR.

An Incident in the Life of the Maternal Great Grandfather of Dr. Livingstone, the African Explorer.

It's no a tale o' luve I sing,
  Nor ane o' war an' glory :
It's juist a lay o' Scottish life—
  A guid auld-warl' story.

Far in the Monklan' muirs langsyne,
  Amang the whins an' heather,
There leev'd an honest, godly man—
  A husband an' a faither.

A hunner years, an' fifty mair,
  Ha'e gane sin' he was leevin';
Sic poortith then as puir men dree't
  We scrimply noo believe in.

Three pennies, maybe four, a day
  The cottar gat for toilin',
In fiel' or fauld, at dyke or sheugh,
  Wi' muckle care an' moilin.

For widows auld an' helpless puir
   Was made but sma' provision,
An' wha cou'd get, an' what they got,
   Was at the kirk's decision.

Short gate frae whaur this guid man leev'd
   There stood a lanely shielin',
Whaur leev'd a widow, auld an' puir,
   That had nae ither bielin'.

Ae saxpence in a month was a'
   Alloo'd her by the session ;
An' to ha'e wished or socht for mair
   Wad been a great transgression.

The honest man weel kenn'd her need,
   An' sae he sent a letter,
An' tauld the minister for shame
   To mak' her something better.

He read the letter owre an' owre,
   Wi' rage maist like to choke—
" Ye craw fu' cruse," quo' he, " I trow
   I'll clip your wings, my cock."

Syne to the toun o' Hamilton
   A letter swith has gane,
That brocht the sodgers up ae nicht,
   An' sae the man was ta'en.

H

They put him up intil the jail,
   Alang wi' mony mae,
And tauld them that they boud to list,
   An' wi' the sodgers gae.

A fearfu' stoun gaed thro' his heart,
   The tear fell frae his e'e,
At thocht o' his dear wife an' bairns,
   Wham he nae mair wad see.

He thocht what holy David did
   Whan he was sair bestead,
An' fleein' frae his ruthless foes,
   He to King Achish fled.

An' whan the sergeant cam' to see,
   An' march his men awa',
He glower'd and blether'd like a fule,
   An' lat his spittle fa'.

The sergeant had a cunning e'e,
   An' sune saw thro' the wile—
Quo' he, " The man's gane oot his min' *
   An' maun be left awhile."

" What is't that brocht ye here," quo' he,
   " What ill thing ha'e ye dune?
I see it's but a feint ye mak',
   Sae tell me true an' sune."

    * Gane oot his min'—lost his reason.

He tauld him sune, he tauld him true—
    "I've dune nae ill ava;
An' oh, I fear my wife an' bairns
    Will starve whan I'm awa'."

"Cheer up, my man," the sergeant said,
    "I'se dae the maist I can
For you: ye've done the thing that's richt,
    Like ony honest man."

Swith to the officer he gaed,
    Was highest in comman'—
Quo' he, "The Monklan' man's gane mad,
    As I can understan'."

"Nae need ha'e we o' madmen here—
    Fie! sen' him swith awa',
Clean oot the gate; it's nocht to me
    Whate'er sall him befa'."

Then back the sergeant cam' wi' speed,
    "Guid news, my frien'," quo' he,
An' put three shillin's in his han',
    "Mak' hameward speedily."

"God bless ye, frien'," the guid man said,
    "Sae muckle gear afore
Has seldom lain within my luif,
    Or yet within my door."

He took the bannet aff his heid
   An' raised to Heaven his e'e—
"The Lord be praised, wha in my need
   Sent sic a frien' to me."

The sergeant lat him through the yett,
   An' shook him by the haun'—
" Fareweel, my frien', we'll meet again
   In yonder happy lan'."

They pairted ne'er to meet on yirth,
   He took the road for hame.
An' whiles he prayed, an' whiles he sang
   Praise to the blessed Name.

The sun gaed doon, the gloamin' fell,
   The nicht was fair an' calm,
Whan he stood on his ain door-stane,
   An' heard the e'enin' psalm

Sung by his wife an' bairns, wha pray'd
   Wi' mony a sab an' tear,
That God wad sen' their faither back—
   They thocht nae he was near.

His heart was duntin' in his breast,
   The tears ran doon his cheek ;
He chappit saftly at the door,
   But oh, he couldna speak.

An' whan the wife cam' to the door,
   A screigh o' joy gied she,
An' fell intil his open arms ;
   Sae did the bairnies three.

An' whan they were come till themsel's,
   " My dearest wife," said he,
" An' you, my bairnies, come an' sit
   Aroun' yer faither's knee.

" Ye raised the psalm in dule an' wae,
   An' prayed wi' sabs an' tears ;
We'll sing a psalm o' joy an' praise
   To Him wha prayer hears."

They sang the psalm wi' joyfu' hearts,
   An' poured the gratefu' prayer ;
Laigh was the roof, an' mean the cot,
   But God himsel' was there.

An' aye at e'en an' mornin' prayer,
   Within that lanely cot,
The faither's Christian sodger frien'
   Was never ance forgot.

ON THE DEATH OF JOHN CASSELL,

THE TRUE AND ESTEEMED FRIEND OF THE WORKING MAN.

WHAT mournful voices thrill upon my ears?
  What wailing tones of sorrow vex the air?
They speak a woe that lies too deep for tears,
  A woe that every son of toil will share.

The mournful voice, the sorrow and the woe
  Are heard, and known, and felt o'er Europe broad;
Cassell is dead! his work is done below—
  He rests upon the bosom of his God!

Friend of the working man! the heart-warm tear,
  Wiped by the horny hand of honest toil,
Is shed in grateful showers upon thy bier,
  By million workmen upon British soil!

Their friend and advocate—the wise and good!
  Their interests ever were with him supreme—
A father working for their mental food—
  Their progress upward, onward, still his theme.

No mythic figures, drooping o'er his dust,
   Can symbolise his virtues and his worth ;
No "storied urn or animated bust"
   Relates his labours, draws his merits forth.

A leader in the van of knowledge still,
   He won his laurels on the field of mind,
In combat keen with ignorance and ill—
   The trophies of his power remain. behind !

ON THE DEATH OF THE

REV. MATTHEW GARDNER, D.D.,

Of Bothwell,

WHO DIED 4TH JUNE, 1865, IN HIS NINETIETH YEAR, AND SIXTY-THIRD OF HIS MINISTRY IN THAT PARISH.

RIPE, fully ripe, then came the reaper Death,
With sickle keen, with cold and withering breath,
And reaped the shock.   The watchful angels near
With songs of joy to Heaven's high garner bear
The golden grain—given to sepulchral earth,
The worn remains await a second birth.

 Gone from our midst, last of the reverned band
 That wont of old in Monkland church to stand,
 To break the bread, and pour the sacred wine,
 Blest symbols of the sacrifice divine,
 With " thoughts that breathed, and words that
  burned," to move
 The eye to tears—the heart to melt in love.

'Tis sixty years since, in the open air,
I heard him first the word of life declare.
Amongst the graves, upon the grassy mounds,
We sat, and raised with heart and voice the sounds

Of sacred psalmody, while wood and plain
Rung answering echoes to the solemn strain.
Then with what unction, with what power and zeal,
Rich gospel balm sin-wounded souls to heal,
" The old man eloquent, with heart and tongue,"
Would pour, while we upon his accents hung !
" Truth from his lips prevailed with double sway "
When calling souls to turn, repent, and pray.

Thus said the Lord—Oh ! faithful and beloved,
Well have the talents given thee been improved—
Well done, thou good and faithful servant, come,
My love, My joys are thine, and "Heaven thy home."

SPUNKIE.

O, WHAT's come o' Spunkie; can naebody tell
Whaur it dances an' blinks at e'en on the fell?
It's lang since I saw the bit flickerin' licht
Skippin' roun' the bog holes an' mosses at nicht.

The lichts o' langsyne are noo laid on the shelf,
An' maybe they've smoor't the wee wannerin' elf,
Or sous'd the bit Spunk in some broun mossy stank,
Sae deep that it canna win up to the bank.

Oor auld faithers thocht that some uncanny thing
Gaed dancin' wi' Spunkie, puir bodies to bring—
Wha tint the richt gate, in the dark howe o' nicht—
Into danger an' dool wi' his cheatrie licht.

A tale aboot Spunkie I here hae to tell,
It was frae my mither's ain lips that it fell:
Her grannie, she said, a guid mither an' wife,
Had followed the imp to the loss o' her life.

On the muir she had wanner't ae misty hairst nicht,
An' saw no far distant a waverin' licht;
That licht is a lamp in some winnock, thocht she,
I wonner wha aughts it, but sune I sall see.

She never cam' hame, but they trackit her feet
To the moss ; it was there wi' death she did meet,
In a boggy well-e'e owre heid she had sunk.
Beguil'd by the licht o' the wannerin' Spunk.

Auld Spunkie's sair wyted for mony misdeeds.
His wild licht ne'er guides us, but aften misleads :
Whan wanner't in darkness an' oot o' the way,
It dances and dazzles to lead us astray.

There's mony a Spunkie that dazzles oor een, ·
An' dances before us to ruin, I ween ;
Tak' tent o' the Spunkie that wilders the brain—
That leads ye to danger, to poortith, an' pain.

There's a licht frae abune, sae steady an' pure,
Sae true, we may follow, frae danger secure ;
That licht never dazzles or leads us astray,
In the darkest o' nichts it shines on the way.

SPRING.

THE wintry storms are over,
  The winds are lull'd to rest ;
Spring is tripping o'er the meads
  With violets on her breast.
The daisy shy is peeping
  Up from the fresh green sod ;
The lark on high is singing
  A hymn of praise to God.

The sportive stream is dancing
  And singing through the dell,
Where children gather cresses
  Beside the fairy well.
Primrose pale and hyacinth blue
  In sweet profusion blow,
And feath'ry ferns are waving
  Around the blossom'd sloe.

Blithesome lambs are gamb'ling
    O'er meadow, lea, and hill,
And minnow shoals are swarming
    In every sunny rill.
The woodland glades are ringing
    With trilling, tuneful notes,
Poured out in love and gladness
    From thousand warbling throats.

Fragrant birch and scented briar
    Are breathing in the breeze,
And May her blossom'd banner hangs
    Upon the hawthorn trees.
Nature in her sweetest mood
    Has sown the earth with flowers—
Drawn from the founts of dew, her hands
    The vernal treasure pours.

How sweet, how pure the pleasure—
    How little understood—
To trace Thy hand in nature,
    Thou Giver of all good!
Thy glory in the sunshine,
    Thy beauty in the flowers,
Thy bounty in the springing corn,
    And balmy April showers.

Nature—fair in every phase,
    The changing seasons bring,
Is fairest in the vernal flush—
    The garniture of Spring.
Hers is the promise of the year,
    The dawn of virgin charms,
The fair young bride soon sleeping
    In Summer's glowing arms.

Summer! lily-crown'd and rich
    In myriad rosy blooms,
Charming the eye, and shedding
    A thousand sweet perfumes—
Yet, queenly Summer! never
    To thee my muse can sing
The strains, so sweet and tender,
    That hail the budding Spring.

BALLAD OF THE NEW MONKLAND MARTYR.

DOCHTER Peggy sat on the kiln,
    An' watch'd owre her faither's life,
For he had been at Both'ell brig,
    An' joined in the bluidy strife.

They socht him air', they socht him late,
    Four lang years an' a day,
But ne'er cou'd fin' the hidin'-place,
    Whaur John o' the Staun he lay.

Aye she span at her rock o' tow,
    An' twirl'd her spin'le free—
Aye she leukit owre muir an' moss
    To see what she micht see.

For faither aft cam' till the hoose,
    An' gat him warm'd an' fed,
An' fain was he to streek him doun,
    An' rest him in his bed.

Dochter Peggy sat on the kiln,
    An', ere she was aware,
Cam' ridin' roun' Pinwinnie wud
    Sax black dragoons, an' mair.

"O ! faither, faither, rin for life,"
   She cried, an' forth he sprang ;
The black dragoons rode to the door,
   An' swords an' bridles rang.

They saw him makin' for the moss—
   Wow, but he ran wi' speed ;
They fired, an' cut the siller saughs,
   That tremil't ower his head.

They durstna ride intil the bog,
   That shoogit aneath their feet ;
He dern'd him in a black moss hag,
   For houkin' oot the peat.

Whan mony a day had come an' gane,
   An' cam' nae mair dragoons,
An' John had maistly tint the fear
   O' the black an' bluidy loons.

"My bairns are wee, my grun lies lea,
   My girnel's toom o' meal,"
Quo' John, "an' I wad yoke the pleugh,
   Gif I durst gang a-fiel'."

He gaed a-fiel', he yokit the pleugh—
   Waeworth that wearifu' day,
For word has gane to the black dragoons,
   In Embro' whaur they lay.

They watch'd a' nicht in Piuwinnie wud,
    An' saw John come a-fiel';
Twa o' them slippit oot on fit,
    An' ahint his back did steal.

Stark an' strang they grippit his arms,
    An' swith the rest cam' on,
Syne trail'd they oot frae 'tween the stilts
    Oor gude an' godly John.

Dochter Peggy stood on the kiln,
    An' turn'd her roun' an' roun'—
The sicht she saw gaed thro' her heart
    Wi' a deep an' deadly stoun.

An' aye she skreigh'd an' aye she ran,
    Wi' feet a' bluidy an' bare;
They rave her oot her faither's arms,
    An' harl'd her by the hair.

Mither an' bairns were sleepin' soun',
    An' nocht kenn'd they ava,
Till Peggy stacher'd on the floor,
    An' swarfin' doun did fa'.

An', lang ere she cou'd tell her tale,
    The faither was aff an' awa;
An' that dear wife, an' bairnies wee,
    He saw nae mair ava.

I

They lows'd a horse frae oot the pleugh,
  An' set him on its back—
Aneath the belly tied his feet,
  An' garr'd the sinnins crack.

They carried him to Embro' toun,
  An' pat him in the jail,
An' weel he kenn'd that he boud dee
  Ere lang, withootin' fail.

An' there they set him to be tried
  Before the men o' bluid;
The holy peace that filled his soul
  They little unnerstude.

He said he was at Both'ell brig,
  An' there he bare a sword,
An' he wad dae the like again
  For Christ, his blessed Lord.

They speer'd at him what was his thocht
  O' Sharpe the bishop's death?
He said, the killer an' the kill'd
  The Lord sall judge them baith.

They bade him pray for gude King James,
  His sovereign lord an' king;
He said it was nae place for prayer,
  Or ony sic-like thing.

An' sae they pass'd the doom o' death
  On John : an' he maun dee
An' hing afore the aul' tolbooth,
  High on the gallows tree.

An' ither twa stude wi' him there ;
  Their sentence was the same ;
Great was their joy to gi'e their lives
  For Christ, his blessed name.

An' whan they were brocht oot to dee,
  John first laid doun his life,
Commendin' weel his soul to God,
  An' eke his bairns an' wife.

In saxteen-aughty-three he died—
  John Whitelaw was his name —
The Monklan' martyr he was ca'd—
  The farm o' Staun his hame.

INTEMPERANCE AND THE SUNDAY TRAINS.

"Oh that my head were waters," and mine eyes
  A tearful fountain, ever running over,
A heart that bleeds, and struggles, moans, and sighs
  O'er thousands slain—whose blood earth may not
    cover.

At corners of the streets, by night and day,
  They stalk, they stagger, fall, and rise no more;
Like festering masses of insensate clay,
  Lie thickly strewn on life's encumbered shore.

Most dread Intemperance, shall it not suffice,
  That, throned and crowned, thou reignest as a queen
In million homes, on British soil that rise,
  Where still thy direful power is felt and seen?

The drunkard's song, the oath, the jest obscene,
  Familiar sounds to us—for ever nigh,
And in our midst, such scenes are often seen
  As shock the soul and blast the gazer's eye.

The huge distillery, ever " bleeding gold,"
    For statesmen's hands to spend or sport away ;
The marts, where souls are bought and spirits sold,
    Are rising, opening, filling day by day.

Say, shall not this, ay, more than this, suffice ?
    The thousand horrors, daily felt and seen !
Say is it not enough, ye good and wise ?
    Then why should newer horrors supervene ?

'Tis Sunday evening, and the twilight gray
    Is fading into night—mid peace profound,
When screaming, rushing, on its iron way,
    The locomotive wakes the echoes round.

They reach the goal, the cars disgorge their fare ;
    Stand close, observe, while they are passing near,
Vile fumes of drink and smoke infest the air,
    And jest and laughter light offend the ear.

A girl is hanging on her sweetheart's arm,
    Who looks into her eyes with maudlin' leer ;
Ah ! parents, little reck ye of the harm
    Done to your children, when you drag them here.

" Oh, this is brave," say you—" now we are free
    To boat or rail—each man to please himself ;
No Sabbatarian hypocrites are we,
    We lay the Fourth Commandment on the shelf."

Blest " pearl of days," now trodden under foot
  By thousands, who would turn again to rend
The hand that gave the jewel, and uproot
  The fences set God's precepts to defend.

Let potsherds strive with potsherds of the earth,
  But woe to him that striveth with his Maker ;
Let such, even now, join trembling with their mirth,
  And in such deeds, my soul, be not partaker.

RETROSPECT OF SONG.

I've sung of Spring, her buds and flowers,
  Of Summer suns and Summer roses ;
Of golden Autumn's dreamy skies,
  The wealth her bounteous reign discloses.

I've sung of Winter, stern and drear,
  His drifting snows and storm blasts chilling ;
Of horrid war's embattled fields,
  And thousands wounded, killed, or killing.

And I have sung, and I have wept,
  O'er one sad theme : O how I shrink
With horror at the foul contact,
  When thou art near me, Belial drink !

And I have hymned fair Nature's praise
  With ardent love and high devotion,
And Garibaldi's hymn, that swells
  Round yon lone islet of the ocean.

The song of liberty I've sung,
  And joined the high triumphant strain,
When she unlocked the dungeon cells,
  And broke Italia's galling chain.

And ah ! how gladly I would join
  The song of peace—the jubilee
Of concord between sister lands,
  When love, not wrath, bids slaves be free.

O ! cease, thou horrid trump of war,
  With brazen clangor loudly blaring,
Arousing all the soul of man
  To deeds of blood and hostile daring.

" Hang ye the trumpet in the hall ;"
  Let brother clasp the hand of brother,
And learn the arts of war no more ;
  All strife and civil discord smother.

" But appetite, I fear, has grown
  By what it feeds on," blood must flow ;
And o'er earth's fairest lands still rolls
  The tide of carnage, spoil, and woe.

May He who rides upon the storm
  Of human passion fierce and strong,
Curb and subdue the demon steeds
  Of civil war !—O Lord, how long ?

"BOTHWELL BRIG."

ON HEARING AN IMPRESSIVE SERMON DELIVERED (SABBATH, JUNE 10TH, 1866) ON THE PLACE WHERE THE BATTLE OF BOTHWELL BRIDGE WAS FOUGHT, COMMEMORATIVE OF THAT EVENT.

O, BONNIE Clyde! a shimmering gleam
  Oot owre thy rippling bosom plays,
Whan frae the bricht blue sky o' June
  The sun leuks doun on simmer days.

But ne'er did glancin' sunbeams glint,
  An' owre thy dancin' waters play
Mair bricht, than whan to "Bothwell Brig"
  We teuk the road ae Sabbath day.

An' ne'er owre "Bothwell banks sae fair,"
  Sae aft by Scottish minstrels sung,
Were wafted higher, holier strains,
  Till bank an' brae wi' echoes rung.

Auld Scotlan's stout an' stalwart sons,
  An' bonnie lasses gather'd there,
An' mithers douce, wi' restless bairns,
  Auld men an' wives wi' siller hair.

An' een grew dim, and hearts were fu',
   As owre the vera grun' they trod,
Whaur their forbears, for conscience sake,
   Had pour'd their life-bluid on the sod.

My granny's gutcher bare a sword
   At Bothwell brig that dolefu' day,
An' ne'er had left the bluidy fiel'
   But for his guid an' gallant grey.

She swam wi' him across the Clyde,
   An' bare him to his ain door stane ;
Lang after that he hidin' lay
   Till he was hunted oot an' ta'en.

For Christ, his croun an' covenant, he
   Laid doon his life in Embro' toun,
An' frae the scaffold rose to wear
   The victor's palm, the martyr's croun.

Noo, God be prais'd, sic times are gane ;
   Let Scots be Scots—they'll ne'er return ;
Nor king nor priest again ha'e power,
   Gude men, an' true, to hang an' burn.

An' noo, frae a' the airts that blaw,
   By thoosan's folk cam' thrangin' in,
An' roun' an' roun' they sat them doun,
   Until the holy wark begin.

They raised the Psalm, it swell'd, it thrill'd,
   It mounted to the gates o' heaven,
An' ne'er mair sweet, mair solemn joy,
   By singin' o' the Psalms was given.

Wi' pleadin' voice, an' words o' power,
   The preacher poured his soul in prayer—
Prayed that the martyrs' covenant God
   Wad bless them wi' His presence there.

An' O ! what witnesses unseen
   May us that day ha'e compass'd round,
Wha loved their lives not to the death,
   An' noo wi' Christ in glory crown'd.

An' bless'd be God, we noo can sit
   Beneath oor vine an' fig tree shade—
May raise the Psalm, an' preach, an' pray,
   Nane daurin' to mak' us afraid.

Wha, noo, frae aff his ain hearth-stane,
   Will drag the husband an' the faither,
Syne leave him to his wife an' bairns
   A bluidy corpse upon the heather?

Nae dark Dalzell, nae Claver'se stern,
   Ride forth wi' sword an' bridle ringin',
Oor sufferin' covenanted sires
   To prison an' the scaffold bringin'.

The memories o' her martyred dead
　　May Scotlan' dearly cherish ever;
They sowed the seed, we reap the grain—
　　Their names, their deeds, shall perish never.

THE ISLES OF GREECE.

AN APPEAL FOR THE CANDIOTES.

"The Isles of Greece! the Isles of Greece!"
   In blood and bondage. Ah, to know,
To find the land, the hand, the brand
   Would lay the turban'd despot low!

I know a land, an ocean isle,
   That can, that would, but may not lend
Her name, her power, ye islemen brave,
   The fetters from your limbs to rend.

Yet she, to Moslem allies true,
   Gave name and power, gave hand and brand,
Gave thousands of her gallant sons
   To perish on the Crimean strand.

"How are the mighty fallen!" Now,
   Each generous impulse we restrain ;
When British freedom walks abroad,
   She drags at foot the clog and chain!

There is a hand that wields a brand,
   That hand unsheathed it never, never,
But to descend, with lightning flash,
   The bonds of tyranny to sever.

O! might that hand unsheath it now,
　And bid it gleam on Ægean waters,
To save for Greece, from Moslem hands,
　The fairest of her sea-born daughters.

It may not be.　Behind the scenes
　Sits old Diplomacy, still weaving
The web of statecraft, made to hide
　"The tricks of state" and cool deceiving.

Yet still that hand, that brand are thine,
　O Garibaldi!　Ever, ever,
That hand is raised, that brand unsheathed,
　The oppressed, the trampled to deliver!

DARK HOURS.

The Drunkard's Mother.

Dark hours of tearless, sleepless grief,
Of woe, denied the soft relief
Of tears, to soothe the burning smart
That throbs and festers in my heart.
Oft has this grief my soul o'erspread,
Like funeral pall above the dead.
Ah, me! beneath the coffin-lid
Of murdered hopes for ever hid,
My promised joys of love and trust
With them lie mouldering in the dust.

    Ah! not in sentimental strain
Of love-sick maid and sighing swain
I sing, who, crossed in hapless love,
The tender anguish deeply prove—
Nor that fierce grief when loss of fame,
Of wealth, of power, the baffled aim
Of worldly schemes, sends to the heart
Keen disappointment's venom'd dart.

    Is such thy grief? you ask.—Ah, no!
A darker, deeper, deadlier woe
Is mine. Within its poisonous folds
My writhing heart a serpent holds;
I vainly struggle in the toils,
More closely wind the crushing coils.

No hand but His, to whom is given
All power in earth, all power in heaven,
The hideous reptile can unwind,
My crushed and broken heart upbind.
    Lord, speak with power, I Thee implore,
As when, by lone Gennesaret's shore,
As God, Thou gave the high command,
That legion fiends might not withstand.
Oh, speak the words of power again,
All power, all words but Thine are vain ;
This demoniac, fiercely driven,
Assaulting man, defying heaven,
'Twere joy ineffable, complete,
To see him sitting at Thy feet,
Renewed in heart, in mind restored,
Oh, speak the word ; oh, save him, Lord !

RHYMES FOR THE TIMES—I., 1865.

This while I've been ettlin' to string a wheen rhymes,
Being unco sair fash'd at the signs o' the times—
The mony dark omens aroun' an' abune,
The upshot o' whilk will be seen on us sune.

The cholera's wan'ering roun' us this while,
An' I watna hoo sune it may come to our isle,
Whan, on Sabbath, instead o' a ride on the rail,
We may follow the deid-cart wi' greeting an' wail.

The pest 'mang oor bestial is spreading like fire,
The sta's are a' toom noo in mony a byre,
The hirsels are dwinin' on hillside an' lea,
An' the grief an' the losses are waesome to dree.

We've lost our gude Premier : I houp he's at rest
In the lan' o' the leal, wi' the gude an' the blest ;
God bless oor wee Johnnie ! he'll dae what he can
For our gude—a true Briton, an' leal heartit man.

K

We're a' to be chawed up by big cousin Sam,
Wha brags he has brocht the dark children o' Ham
Out the hoose o' their bondage, an' set them a' free;
May they use weel the blessin'!—belyve we sall see.

A plague's rife amang us that bears aye the bell:
It's the plague o' intemperance—what mortal may tell
How fearfu' the curse an' the plague-sairs how foul,
That poison the body and ruin the soul!

THE MAY FLOWER.

VERSES INSCRIBED TO A VERY DEAR FRIEND, WHO PRESENTED ME WITH A
BEAUTIFUL BRANCH OF THE "MAY FLOWER," OR HAWTHORN BLOSSOM.

MAY, sweet May! this branch of blossom
From thy fragrant, beauteous bosom,
I accept and clasp the treasure
To my breast with grateful pleasure.

Dear the gift, and dear the giver,
Whose loving hand is near me ever
To shield from care—the mother ailing,
To cheer her heart and spirits failing.

Thanks, sweet May! thy gift I cherish,
Soon, alas! too soon to perish;
Though a thing of beauty, never
Canst thou be a joy for ever.

Thy snowy blossoms freshly blooming,
With their odorous breath perfuming
The chamber small, where still I treasure
Thy floral gift, sweet May! with pleasure.

I press them to my cheek, inhaling
Sweet nature's incense, still exhaling
From thy verdant lap o'erflowing
With flow'ry blooms, bright hued and glowing.

Branch of May! the dews of morning
Twinkle on thy leaves, adorning
The pearly blooms that richly cluster
On each spray with sparkling lustre.

Ere from parent tree dissever'd,
Wood-notes rung and bright wings quiver'd
Through the branches—every blossom
Brush'd by some soft feathery bosom.

The songster thrush, the blackbird mellow,
The black-capp'd bullfinch, dear bright fellow,
There build, and brood, and warble clearly;
They haunt and love the hawthorn dearly.

Now the sun of June uncloses
The fragrant treasures of the roses:
Queenly flower, soft, balmy blushing!
The glen, the grove, with beauty flushing.

Onbank and mead, in copse and wildwood,
Wilding flowers, beloved from childhood,
In sweet profusion greet me smiling,
Cares and toils, and tears beguiling.

Memory ever fondly clinging
To the past, before me bringing,
With deepest sweetest fascination,
Past scenes of love and admiration.

Sweet May, adieu! Oh! not in sorrow,
Though now a night, that knows no morrow.
Broods on my eyes; yet I, resigning
My will to heaven, live unrepining.

IMPORTANT QUERIES.

Why this hurrying to and fro,
  Why all this strange commotion?
The good ship Briton rolls and sways
  Upon a stormy ocean.
Oh! where the skilful pilot's hand
  To steer her through the breakers?
Or must she drift till, on the strand,
  She lies the prey of wreckers?

Oh! why this running to and fro:
  Is knowledge true increasing?
When human knowledge leads the van
  The true is oft decreasing.
The newer lights, so vaunted now,
  The learning of the college,
The lights of science unbaptized—
  Lead they to saving knowledge!

Oh! why this running to and fro,
    The fiery demon chasing;
The Moloch spirit of the still
    With deadly clasp embracing?
Dread spirit, at thy burning shrine
    Are we still sacrificing
Our all on earth, our hopes in heaven—
    All—all—yet not sufficing?

Ah, mothers! why this sad neglect
    Of due maternal training—
Guarding the young from speech profane—
    From evil deeds restraining?
Why prove yourselves unfit to use
    Your true and high vocation—
To teach and train the young who form
    The future generation?

Why ever running to and fro,
    Eschewing the reflection
That household cares and children's weal
    Demand your close inspection?
'Tis not enough they go to school
    And enter through the portals—
The faithful mother caters lore
    To suit her young immortals.

Oh ! why so oft by vice and sloth
  Make home unclean, unholy,
Where children pine in rags and want—
  A sight most melancholy ;
Where boys and girls grow up untaught,
  Uncared for, and untended,
Their future lives a dreary waste
  Of sin and misery blended ?

Why ever running to and fro
  Are children shouting, playing,
Upon the Sabbath ?—Mothers, why
  Your sacred trust betraying ?
Have you no thought of guilt incurr'd
  While you are not restraining
Their childish sports in field and street,
  The holy day profaning ?

Oh, working mothers ! list my rhymes,
  'Tis you I am addressing—
The workman's home and hearth are yours
  For either bane or blessing.
God bless and help you to fulfil
  The duties of your station !
These duties, well performed, will raise,
  Adorn and bless the nation.

WILD FLOWERS.

THE fragrant dewy rose,
    The lily pure and pale,
Each flower the garden shows,
    To charm my spirit fail;
Their beauties I admire,
    Their fragrance I inhale—
Flowers of my fond desire,
    Ye bloom in wood and vale!

I love the tender bloom
    On Nature's blushing face--
The violet's soft perfume,
    The cowslip's drooping grace:
The hyacinth's azure bells,
    Primrose in paley gold,
Starring the woody dells,
    And gemming mead and wold;

Laburnum wreaths of gold.
　　Accacia blossoms white,
Rho'dendron's crimson fold,
　　All beauteous to the sight;
The lilac soft and fair,
　　Green laurel's glossy sheen—
My heart will not compare
　　With Scotia's shrubs, I ween.

How fair the milk-white thorn,
　　How rich her fragrant breath
On evening breezes borne!
　　How sweet the blooming heath—
Old Scotia's emblem dear—
　　In regal purple dress'd!
Her fragrant bells I wear
　　With pride upon my breast.

The eglantine that winds
　　Her slender flowery arms
Round some hoar trunk, and binds
　　The sense with honey'd charms;
And sweeter, fairer still,
　　The flush of wilding roses,
That Nature's own sweet will
　　In copse and dell discloses.

WILD FLOWERS.

I love the bonnie broom,
  Whose golden tresses play
O'er the mead where daisies bloom,
  And maidens come to May!
I love thee, land of mine—
  Thy every shrub and flower
I in my heart enshrine,
  And with my love endower!

TO THE REV. JOHN JAMES,

On his going out to Canada.

Arise, for this is not thy rest; go forth
And brave the frozen rigours of the north ;
Though cold the clime, the hearts are warm and true.
That prompt the genuine welcome waiting you.
May He, whom even the winds and waves obey,
Thee safe across the wint'ry seas convey ;
And though the angry ocean roll and swell,
May peace divine within thy bosom dwell :
And thou a sore-tossed barque, the tempest past,
Find a quiet haven of repose at last.
A door is shut—a more effectual door
May open to thee—to be shut no more
By men, who strain at gnats, and swallow camels,
And clog the preached Word with useless trammels ;
Who, while they anise, mint, and cumin gather,
Prefer Church etiquette, light as a feather
With weightier matters of the law compared,
Even judgment, mercy, truth ! Ah, thou hast shared
The woes of hope deferred, but not the woe
Of those who said, Ah ! we would have it so.
Well, they have had their way ; it little mattered
To them that thus the little flock was scattered—

The fold shut up—the shepherd gone away—
The flock dispersed.   What need we more to say ?
My friend, may God thy refuge be and strength,
In all thy wanderings guide thee, till at length
He bring thee, by His providential grace,
Through fire and water to a wealthy place.
The partner of thy cares, thy hope, thy life,
Thy loved, thy tried, thy true and suffering wife,
And all the youthful loving ones that cling
Around her knees, may God in safety bring
Soon to the father's clasping arms again,
United in one home beyond the main.
Though strong the filial ties that bind thy heart,
The hour is come, again thou must depart ;
The parent's blessing, and their last farewell
Shall long in memory's sacred records dwell.
'Tis sad to part with those who have with thee
Lain in the bosom, smiled upon the knee
Of one fond mother.   From the womb of time
May spring a blest reunion ; every clime,
Earth's utmost bounds, in all beneath the sky,
His presence, power, and love are ever nigh.
   Farewell ! my friend, farewell ! in all thy ways
Commit thyself to Him ; thou yet shall praise
Him for the way he led thee.   To the end
His presence go with thee.   Farewell, my friend !

RHYMES FOR THE TIMES—II., 1865.

Juist noo there are mony wha rin to an' fro,
An' knowledge increases, abune an' below;
The yird's like a riddle, pits, tunnels, an' bores,
Whaur bodies, like mowdies, by hunners an' scores.
Are houkin', an' holin', an' blastin' the rocks;
An' droonin's an' burnin's, explosions an' shocks,
An' a' ither meagries, amang us are rife:
Oh, mony's the slain in the battle o' life!
It's Mammon we worship, wi' graspin' an' greed,
Wi' sailin' an' railin' at telegraph speed,
Get gowd oot the ironstane, an' siller frae coal,
An' thoosan's on thoosan's draw oot o' a'e hole.
Wi' oil shale aneath us, an' fire-warks abune,
I think we'll tak' lowe, an bleeze up to the mune.
The kintra's contentit' an' hale at the heart;
That gleg birkie, Gladstone, has weel dune his part:
Exchequer's big pouches o' siller are fu',
An' mony's the taxes that's dune awa' noo;
An' labour's weel paid, an' the flour an' the meal
At a wanworth—an' sae we micht fen unco weel.
Oor Premier has promised to stan' for reform;
The Fins an' the Yankees are brewin' a storm.
They're swallin' an' frothin' wi' bunkum an' bosh.
But they daurna come near oor bit islan' sae cosh.

There's a bee in the bannet o' some o' the cloth,
The Sabbath's the subject, an' wow but I'm wroth
To see the blin' leaders lead blin' men awa',
Till into the ditch they baith stummle an' fa'.
"The soul is immortal," tak' that for a text,
"The body is perishin'," tak' for the next;—
To whilk o' the twa shou'd the Sabbath be given?
To the body?—then what for the soul an' for heaven?

BRAVE ANGUS CAMERON,

THE WINNER OF THE QUEEN'S PRIZE AT RIFLE SHOOTING, WIMBLEDON, 1866.

"When wine and other liquors were pressed upon him after he was proclaimed victor, he refused to partake of anything save a draught of ginger-beer, he being a strict teetotaller."

BRAVE Cameron, it needs not the lore of the seer,
In this the bright dawn of thy youthful career,
To tell what the future for thee has in store,
" For coming events cast their shadows before."

Brave Cameron, 'twas not on the red field of fight,
Where death-shots are pealing and swords gleaming
  bright,
'Twas where wine-cups were brimmed for the lord of
  the prize,
The gift of Victoria, the good and the wise.

Brave Cameron, full well was thy courage envinced
In a scene where the bravest have faltered and winced,
When true to thy pledge and thy principles high,
When the wine-cup was proffered thou motioned it by.

Brave Cameron, true Cameron, thy country, I ween,
With pride thy rare skill as a marksman has seen;
More dearly she greets thee, young, gallant, and true,
Unscathed by an ordeal borne bravely by few:

Brave Cameron, through life be thou ever the same,
Unfailing in practice, unerring in aim,
Unswerving in principle, honour, and truth,
Thy laurels in age be as green as in youth!

LINES

Summer, long, and bright, and glowing,
Flowers in triple plenty blowing,
Flushed the garden, field and glade,
Tints of every hue and shade.
Woods and fields more richly green,
Waters placid, pure and sheen,
Singing, sparkling, danced along,
Musical as merles' song.
Ne'er did "incense breathing morn"
O'er green fields of springing corn,
Flowery lea, and moorland heath,
Shed more balmy odorous breath.
Such pearl-drops ne'er, I ween,
Gathered were on village green,
On sweet May, by sportive girls,
They the purest, fairest pearls,
'Sixty-five as thou hast given
From the dewy morning heaven.
With the first faint streak of morn,
When the cock first winds his horn,
Wakes the music of the woods,
Rising, swelling into floods

Of melody !   Sweet warbling throats !
How ye poured your jubilant notes
Of love and joy, devoid of fear :
No tuneless Winter chilled your cheer.
   In that Summer, long and glowing,
Nature from her lap o'erflowing
Spread around an ample feast
With full hand for bird and beast.
Ah ! what pleasure 'twas to see
Straying o'er the daisied lea,
Or, recumbent on the sward,
"The milky mothers of the herd,"
Udder rich in lacteal wealth,
Full of lusty life and health—
Richest clover, greenest grass,   ·
Cropping quietly.
              Now, alas !
Sore plague-smitten, dying, dead,
On the pastures where they fed !
Thousands upon thousands gone—
Deep the loss, and sad the moan
In the dairies and the farms,
Where each day brings fresh alarms :
And the wonder ever grows
Whence the dire distemper flows.
Ah ! not now the milkmaid's song,
As she drives the herd along,
Comes on woodland echoes borne,
At gloamin' grey or dewy morn.

Now she walks with mournful tread
Through each empty stall and shed;
Meets her ear no welcome low:
All is deathly silence now.
For your suff'rings, sinless things,
Weeps the muse even while she sings:
Guilt not yours brought down the rod
Of a just and righteous God.
To that God we now appeal:
He has wounded, He can heal;
He alone can grant release
From this dark and fell disease.
From our sinful, suff'ring land,
Lord, remove Thy chast'ning hand!

GRANNIE'S TALE.

A BALLAD O' MEMORIE.

THE days o' langsyne, O! the days o' langsyne,
Sweet thochts o' the bygane, I never sall tyne ;
Tho' darklin' I sit in my muckle arm chair,
Aul' places, aul' faces, I see them a' there.

O, lanely Blackhill ! nae sun-picture can gi'e
Sae faithfu' a likeness as I ha'e o' thee :
It was ta'en whan the sun o' young memorie was bricht,
An' set in my heart in a crystal o' licht.

In the lang winter nichts, whan a bairn, I wad sit
Wi' my taes in the ase at grannie's wheel-fit,
An' the croon o' her sang, an' the birr o' her wheel,
I ne'er heard the music I likit sae weel.

She sang o' Gill Morice, an' young Gregor's ghost,
The twa bonnie babes in the wud that were lost,
An' Bothwell's fair dochter, the young Leddy Jean,
That was droon'd in the Clyde ae weird hallowe'en.

Sae waesome, sae saft, an' sae sweet was the strain,
That I kenn'd na if maist it was pleasure or pain
That moisten'd my een, an' dirled my heart,
But noo, whan I think on't, they baith had a pairt.

My grannie believed in nae cantrip or spell;
'Bout ghaist, witch, or fairy, nae tale wad she tell;
Sic things by douce bodies, she said, were ne'er seen,
An' they hae little gumption that trow them, I ween.

She had heard, she had seen, an' thocht for hersel',
An' sae she had mony true stories to tell;
But ane she aye tauld wi' the tear in her e'e,
That story I'll min' till the day that I dee.

Said grannie, " Whan I was a lass in my teens,
Ne'er thinkin' what pinchin' or poverty means,
There leev'd, within cry o' my ain faither's door,
A cottar, his wife, wi' their young bairnies four.

On a saxpence a day, in times o' dear meal.
Sax bodies, ye ken, coudna fen unco weel,
But the mither, the best an' the maist o't wad mak',
Tho' whiles the poor bairnies a mealtith wad lack.

Aye patient, an hopefu', an' cheerfu', the wife
Wad never be beat in the battle o' life;
But the man he wud murmur, an' say in his min'
That Providence never to him had been kin'.

An sae whan the fifth ane, a sweet lassie bairn,
Was laid in his arms, he was sairly forfairn;
Nae kin' kiss o' welcome he offer'd to gi'e,
Tho' the puir mither watch'd wi' the tear in her e'e.

The very neist day their aul' laddie, wee Tam,
Wi the caul' an' the weet whan biggin' a dam
Across a bit syke, took a stoppin' o' breath,
On the fourth day was laid in the caul' arms o' death.

An' syne the neist brither, the cantie wee Rabbie,
The mither's ain pet, aye sae steerin an' gabbie,
Was droon'd in the burn; he was waidin' alane
Whaur naebody saw till the life it was gane.

The neist were twin lassies; the sma'-pox had gane
Roun' the hale kintra-side, the twasum were ta'en;
It was muckle they dree'd, but three days atween,
Frae ae bed to ae grave were carried, I ween.

But oh, the puir mither! hoo fen'd she the while?
She was worn oot wi' watchin', wi' sorrow, an' toil;
For want o' things needfu' her bosom was dry,
An' the wee greetin' wean gat little supply.

She lay on the bed that she rose frae nae mair,
The heart-stricken faither leuk'd roun' in despair;
His bairnies were gane, an' the mither wad gang,
An' lie doon beside them before it was lang.

He sat by her bed, an' he sat a' alane,
Her caul' haun in his, till the breath it was gane,
Whan grannie cam' in : she had aften been there
To help them, an' tend them, an' cheer their despair.

Frae the dead mither's side he lifted the wean;
On its face an' wee haunies the tears fell like rain :
God bless thee an' spare thee, my mitherless bairn ;
A gude, but sair lesson, thou'st gi'en me to learn.

' Oh, Jenny !' he said, 'I hae something to say,
That I never ha'e tauld till this sorrowfu' day ;
O' the gudeness o' God a while I had doot—
In this I hae sinn'd, an' my sin's faund me oot.

Whan I first saw this bairnie the nicht she cam' hame,
I said in my heart, to my sin an' my shame,
Whan the cravin' wee mouthie it open'd to greet,
Anither mouth sent me, but whaur is the meat ?

But, oh ! I am punish'd richt sune an' richt sair,
My bairns are a' gane, an' the mither lies there,
Nane left but this wee cravin' mouthie to eat.
Oh ! whaur are the mouths noo, for there is the meat?'

Wi' her e'en fu' o' tears, an' heart fu' o' wae,
My grannie stood still till the man had his say ;
She keek'd in the bed wi' a face like a clout,
Syne ran for some neibours, wha laid the corse oot.

A kin' wific cam', an' said, 'Gi'e me the wean,
I'll think I hae twins, for I've ane o' my ain.'
An' the mitherless lamb at her bosom was fed,
An' like her ain bairnie was cared for an' clad.

Lang years afterhen, on the gowanie sward,
That happit a grave in Cam'nethan kirkyard,
There sat an aul' man—he was seen ilka year.
In that grave lay his wife an' four bairnies dear."

THE DESERTED MANSION.

Damp and drear the lonely halls,
Faint the misty sunlight falls
Through the casement, soil'd and dim,
In the chambers, grey and grim.
On the once-fair-pictured wall
Spiders hang, and reptiles crawl:
Dust lies thick upon the floor,
Through the sounding corridor
Wailing, weird-like echoes swell,
Ringing desolation's knell.
    Where the waxen tapers' blaze
Shone upon the jocund maze,
Where, on "light fantastic toe,"
Dancers tripped it to and fro
To soft music's 'trancing strains,
Darkness now and silence reigns.
Wintry rains, with drip and plash,
Beat upon the mouldering sash,
Through each paneless crevice leaking.
On its broken hinges creaking
Rudely, swung by every blast;
Yet its tells of glories past.
Passing from the drawing-room,
Redolent of soft perfume,

Manly worth and maiden grace,
Through the bright and ample space,
Walked into a world of flowers—
Fair as bloomed in Eden's bowers.
Where the lovely blossoms now?
Ne'er to wreathe young beauty's brow,
Twine amid her shining hair,
Shall they gather blossoms there.
　　Many, many years are gone
Since that mansion, drear and lone,
Was the home of love and gladness,
Seldom dimm'd by lowering sadness.
But, alas! there came a time
When a foul and fearful crime
In that home was perpetrated.
Thus tradition hath it stated:—
Heirs had fail'd.　Of all the line
Lived one orphan girl of nine—
Heiress sole of the domain;
But her guardian would obtain,
If the little maiden died,
What her life to him denied.
In the room that saw her birth,
Placed upon the marble hearth,
Stood one night a poisoned cup—
When he bade, she drank it up.
Ere his matin song the lark
Pour'd, the child lay cold and dark.

On that marble hearth remain,
Since that night the poison stain—
One dark circle, where was placed
The deadly cup.   Ne'er effaced
Shall it be by mortal hand:
Token of the crime it stands.

Now I leave these halls of gloom,
Leave the horror-haunted room,
Out to breathe the balmy air,
Ah, the scene is very fair!
'Tis the glowing summer tide,
See the sparkling waters glide ;
Gushing, singing as they flow
Through the lovely glen below.
Ah, what wealth of wilding flowers,
Wealth of blossom'd hawthorn bowers,
Where a thousand warblers sing
Till the glen's sweet echoes ring.

But the west begins to burn,
From the river's bank I turn,
Musing on my homeward way
On the teachings of the day.

THE DOOM OF THE PAPACY.

BLOW the trumpet, sound the doom,
Let the awful clangours boom
Through high heaven and earth below,
Through the gloomy realms of woe;
Through the caverns of the dead
Let the thunder tones be sped;
Million voices, loud replying,
Shout, the Papacy is dying!

Hark! in heaven the martyr throng,
Crying, Lord, how long, how long,
Till our blood avenged shall be,
Till the earth Thy judgments see?
Wait ye for a little space,
Some who yet on earth have place,
Brother martyrs yet shall be,
Vengeance full ye then shall see,
Vengeance full on Papal Rome,
Vengeance coming, soon to come!
Lo! the herald angel stands.
Poising in his mighty hands
A millstone, emblem of her doom;—
Loud the wrathful thunders boom,
At the mighty angel's call:
Thus shall Rome for ever fall,

As this mighty stone is thrown
Into ocean depths unknown;
Fallen, sunk, for evermore,
In a sea without a shore.

Hark! in heaven a cry again
From the souls of martyr'd slain:
Now the doom of Rome is fixed,
Now the draught of vengeance mixed,
Brimm'd the bitter, burning cup,
She shall surely drink it up.

Loud responding to the skies
Joyful shouts from earth arise;
Now is come salvation, strength,
And the weight of blood at length—
Blood of saints and martyrs blest—
Loads no more her groaning breast;
From the loathed incubus free,
Joins in Heaven's high jubilee.

From abodes of endless woe,
Swift as lightning currents flow,
Rolls the knell of Papal Rome.
Ah! they cry, Art thou become
Like to us?   We greet thee well,
Like to us thou here shalt dwell,
Sunk for aye beneath the load
Of martyr-blood—the doom'd of God.

From your bloody graves awake,
Ye who have for conscience sake
Shed your blood, and spent your breath,
Loved your lives not to the death!
Hear, ye sleepers in the dust!
God, the Avenger, true and just,
Now for blood makes inquisition;
Full and stern the requisition
He will make on bloody Rome.
Strike her knell!—her hour is come!

Sound again the trump of doom
Through the dread and solemn gloom;
Hear again the angel's call,
Rome is doomed—behold her fall!

A LAY OF THE TAMBOUR FRAME.

Bending with straining eyes
   Over the tambour frame,
Never a change in her weary routine—
   Slave in all but the name.
Tambour, ever tambour,
   Tambour the wreathing lines
Of 'broidered silk, till beauty's robe
   In rainbow lustre shines.

There, with colourless cheek;
   There, with her tangling hair;
Still bending low o'er the rickety frame,
   Seek, ye will find her there.
Tambour, ever tambour,
   With fingers cramped and chill;—
The panes are shattered, and cold the wind
   Blows over the eastern hill.

Why quail, my sisters, why,
  As ye were abjects vile,
When begging some haughty brother of earth
  " To give you leave to toil ?"
It is tambour you must,
  Naught else you have to do ;
Though paupers' dole be of higher amount
  Than pay oft earned by you.

No union strikes for you ;—
  Unshielded and alone,
In the battle of life—a battle it is,
  Where virtue is oft o'erthrown.
O working men ! O why
  Pass ye thus careless by,
Nor give to the working woman's complaint
  One word of kind reply ?

Selfish, unfeeling men !
  Have ye not had your will ?
High pay, short hours ; yet your cry, like the leech,
  Is, Give us, give us still.
She who tambours—tambours
  For fifteen hours a day—
Would have shoes on her feet, and dress for church,
  Had she a third of your pay.

M

Sisters, cousins, and aunts
    Are they; yet, if not so,
Say, are they not sisters by human ties,
    And sympathy's kindly flow?
To them how dear the boon
    From brother's hand that came!
It would warm the heart and brighten the eyes,
    While bending o'er the frame.

Raise ye a fund to aid
    In times of deep distress;
While man helps man, to their sisters in need
    Brothers can do no less.
Still the tambourer bends
    Wearily o'er the frame.
Patterns oft vary, for fashions will change—
    She is ever the same.

THE OLD CHURCHYARD.

Lone field of graves! our churchyard old and hoar!
· Trench'd deep, and sown by Death with mortal grain;
Decayed, and dead it lies—not evermore!
  All, all shall live, shall rise to life again!

With ling'ring step, in solemn, musing mood,
  I pass within the time-worn lichen'd walls;
A softened awe steals o'er me as I brood
  On scenes and forms that memory still recalls.

My dreamy eyes, dim with unconscious tears,
  Gaze sadly on a small enclosèd space:
A wild-rose brier its tender greenery rears,
  And sheds its fragrant blossoms o'er the place.

Within that space my sainted mother sleeps;
  Her grandchild's grandchild slumbers at her feet;
One grave the mortal relics safely keeps
  Of five fair infants—sinless, pure, and sweet,

I stand beside a new-made grave: the grass
  Hath not yet greened the dark-brown burial sod—
A wife and mother lies below! Alas!
  With bleeding feet life's thorny path she trode.

Here lies a father. Ah! the toiling hand,
　　The warm paternal heart, and thoughtful brain,
Toil, throb, and think no more. The silent land
　　Gives back no echo to the world again.

A granite tablet here records the worth,
　　The virtues of a man, esteemed, beloved ;
Want, death, and sickness ever called him forth,
　　And vice before him ever stood reproved.

And she, a help-meet true for many years,
　　Beside him lies. Ah! when she was removed,
Deep was our loss, and mourned with many tears—
　　A mother she in Israel well approved.

The scorched and mangled victims of the mine,
　　Full many sleep beneath these lowly mounds:
And crushed, dismembered forms, slain on the line,
　　Find space within their dark and narrow bounds.

Now, on a broad and lettered stone I sit,
　　The gloaming shadows have begun to fall,
Old forms and faces round me seem to flit—
　　They come, they come at brooding fancy's call.

Ah! well I know these patriarchal forms—
　　Our village fathers in the days of yore,
Through humble life, its battles and its storms,
　　Their part they bravely, uncomplaining, bore.

And dames, in coif and 'kerchief, wrinkled, gray,
   Who each the burden, heat, and toils of life,
In poverty along life's flinty way
   Still meekly bore, as daughter, mother, wife.

Sad spirit eyes! why gaze ye on me so,
   The sole survivor of my young compeers?
Six joyous girls we deemed not soon to know,
   "Our happy valley" one long vale of tears.

The dews of evening fall, my dream is o'er;
   The airy phantoms fly, I gaze around,
Nought meets the eye save graves and tombstones hoar,
   And silence reigns, unbroken and profound.

These frail mementoes of mediæval times,
   That still have place upon the crumbling wall,
The open graves, the mournful, funeral chimes,
   The griefs, the tears of centuries past recall.

Lone field of graves, farewell! old churchyard hoar!
   I go, but must and will return again!
I come, but may not go as heretofore;
   Till time and death shall die, with thee remain.

ELEGIAC VERSES:

INSCRIBED, AND SACRED TO THE MEMORY OF THE REV. DR. JOHN
CAMPBELL, OF LONDON, WHO DIED MARCH 26, 1867.

OH, faithful unto death ! thy work is done;
Thy course is finished, and the goal is won;
Thy warfare ended, the reward is given—
A crown of life, the victor's palm in Heaven.

A warrior on the battle-field of life,
When truth and error met in mortal strife,
'Twas his to wield with power the Spirit sword,
And conquer in the battles of the Lord.

From superstition's thrall to free the mind,
The galling chains of slav'ry to unbind,
The Word of God, untrammelled and unbound,
Diffusing free as air the world around.

For this, with zeal that would not swerve or turn,
He strove, " while thoughts that breathe and words
    that burn "
Flashed from his pen, and glowed upon the page —
The beacon light of truth from age to age.

The stroke was sudden, and the tidings came
Swift flashing from the south on wings of flame.
A standard-bearer for the truth lies low;
The Church of Christ hath deeply felt the blow.

His works, his worth, the prestige of his name,
To sorrowing friends most dear, have spread his fame
O'er Europe broad, and many a distant land—
Far ocean isles, on many a coral strand.

A humble friend inscribes this tribute small
To his blest memory.   Grateful tear-drops fall
Upon the page.   Be still, my heart, and know
He rests with God.   His work is done below.

NEWSPAPER FINDINGS, 1867.

Quiet an' cozie, but an' ben,
Sittin' at my ain fire-en',
On the twa-leav'd volume porin',
News baith hame an' foreign storin',
Owre them thinkin', wonnerin', grievin',
Hech, sirs! what a warl' we leeve in!

There's that restless ghaist Reform,
Like a chronic thunner-storm
Roun' the sky politic rummlin',
Gloomin', flashin', ever grummlin'—
Ever mair the auld, auld story,
Nocht worth while frae Whig or Tory.

Shaftesbury! thee oor hearts are thankin'
Noo, whan slavery's chains are clankin',
No on niggers in the south,
But on gangs o' English youth—
Serfs wha suffer, sin, an' toil,
On free Englan's happy soil;
In their cause, thou lead'st the van,
Christian! true, brave Englishman!

Oh! the horrors, crimes, an' pain,
That our social system stain!
Drink's amaist the source o' a'
The countless ills that life befa';
Murders, suicides, an' death,
To the saul an' body baith;
Frae this burnin' scourge we shrink,
Britain's shame, accursèd drink!

Say, has England's kirk become
Mither nurse to Papal Rome?
For her nursery she caters
Fledglin's frae their "Alma Maters."
Kirks they get—O sad reflection!
Sune there's Romish genuflexion—
Altar, can'les, bowin', crossin',
Papistry wi' little glossin'—
Nocht but Romanisèd mummery.
Ah, this ritualistic flummery!
Renegades—I'd gar them 'lop
Hame to Rome an' faither Pope.

Lang there's been a great ado—
Muckle cry, an' little woo'—
'Bout the Union o' the Free
Wi' that thrivin' sect U.P.
Shou'd they join, amalagmation
Shou'd be written conflagration.

Head, an' heart, an' een are sair,
Else I micht sae muckle mair—
Speak o' Bismarck's famous needle,
Tell hoo Nap the Russ can wheedle.
He likesna Teuton Will ava;
Nae luve's lost atween the twa.
Will is auld, maun sune decease,
Sae its best to keep the peace—
Die aggression and ambition
At the Paris Exhibition.

THE WARNING WAIL.

A MINSTREL old, in feudal hall,
    When wassail bowls were brimm'd and flowing,
Responsive to his chieftain's call,
    And joyous dame, young, bright, and glowing,

With harp high strung, with voice of song
    He came,— bright eyes were on him beaming,
And poured the tuneful tide along,
    With eye of fire, and white locks streaming.

He sang of love, of war, and fame,
    At first with harp and voice unfailing:
But with the closing notes there came
    Deep tones of woe and mournful wailing.

I may not wake my harp again,
    He said, to glory, love, and gladness;
Oh, hear ye not each joyous strain
    Dies in a wail of funeral sadness!

Fill up the bowl, hold revel high,
    Even till the lark shall bid good-morrow;
The revel ends not so, they cry,
    The closing wail of coming sorrow.

I sang the bridegroom, while his bride
　　Wore on her brow the orange blossom ;
He gazed on her with tender pride,
　　And fondly drew her to his bosom.

And still I sang in glowing strain
　　Of wedded love too soon to languish;
Then sank my song in moans of pain,
　　And died away in tones of anguish.

And I have sung soft cradle songs
　　Beside my rosy infant sleeping ;
He lived to crush my heart with wrongs,
　　And drown my song in sobs and weeping.

No more, no more!—Be hushed the song,
　　The strain that dies in tones of wailing;
Oh, why the mournful strain prolong
　　On one sad theme so unavailing?

The bard who woke with heart and song
　　High strains of wassail, love, and gladness,
And heard with awe the chords among,
　　A wail of more than mortal sadness.

He deemed a spirit's hand had swept
　　The chords, the sudden doom foretelling
Of his high chieftain, honour'd, wept,
　　Or her, the love-light of his dwelling.

More deep, more dread the wail of woe,
 The spirit-echo of my numbers,
The haunting voice too well I know,
 'Tis his—the fiend that never slumbers.

The cradle hymns, the bridal song,
 Oft sung in strains soft, true and tender ;
The demon comes, the strain ere long
 But tones of wailing woe can render.

The haunting fiend whose voice of fear
 Is in our midst for ever swelling ;
All that is tender, good, and dear,
 From thousand hearts and homes expelling.

How sad the wail when life has fled !
 Yet words and tones of deeper sorrow
Are wailing o'er the living dead,
 Word or wail I need not borrow.

Up to heaven a cry has gone,
 Mourning, woe, and lamentation ;
The chains are thine in which we groan,
 Dread demon of Intoxication.

We see the flood-gates opened wide,
 We see ten thousand victims floating
Upon the foul and turbid tide,
 And licensed vultures o'er them gloating.

They wider still the flood-gates throw,
  To let the red infernal river
O'er all the land in torrents flow ;
  Shut ye the flood-gates, never ! never !

EFFIE—A BALLAD.

SHE was wearin' awa'! she was wearin' awa'!
Wi' the leaves in October, we thocht she wad fa',
For her cheek was owre red, an' her e'e was owre bricht,
Whaur the saul leukit oot like an angel o' licht.

She dwelt in the muirlan's amang the red bells
O' the sweet hinny heather that blooms on the fells,
Whaur the peesweep an' plover are aye on the wing,
An' the lilt o' the lav'rock's first heard in the Spring.

As black as a craw, an' as saft as the silk,
Were the lang locks that fell on a neck like the milk;
She was lithesome an' lo'esome as lassie micht be,
An' saft was the love-licht that danc'd in her e'e.

Puir Effie had lov'd; a' the hopes an' the fears,
The plagues an' the pleasures, the smiles an' the tears
O' love she had kenn'd—she had gane thro' them a'
For fause Jamie Crichton—O' black be his fa'!

The auldest o' five, whan a lassie o' ten,
She had baith the hoose an' the bairnies to fen';
The mither had gane whan she was but a bairn,
Sae Effie had mony sad lessons to learn.

At hame, had ye seen her amang the young chips,
The sweet law o' kindness was aye on her lips;
She kamed oot their hair, wash'd their wee hackit feet,
Wi' sae tentie a haun that a bairn wadna greet.

She was to her faither the licht o' his een,
He said she wad be what her mither had been—
A fair an' sweet sample o' true womanhood,
Sae carfu' an' clever, sae bonnie an' guid,

The cot-house it stood on the lip o' the burn,
That wimpled an' jinkit wi' mony a turn
Roun' the fit o' the heather-fring'd gowany brae,
Whaur the ae cow was tether'd, an bairnies at play.

Sweet Effie was juist in the midst o' her teens
Whan she gat the first inkling o' what wooing means
Frae a chiel in the clachan, wha aften was seen
Stealin' up the burnside to the cot-hoose at e'en.

On a saft simmer gloamin' I saw them mysel'
On the bank o' the burnie, an' weel I cou'd tell,
By the hue on her cheek, an' the blink o' her e'e,
That her young love was his, an' wad evermair be.

Belyve to fair Effie cam' wooers galore,
An' mony saft tirlin's at e'en on the door;
She smiled on them a', but gied welcome to nane—
Her first love an' last was young Jamie's alane.

An' Jamie, wha ne'er was a week frae her side,
Had vowed e'er a towmond to mak' her his bride;
Her troth she had gi'en him wi' blushes an' tears—
It was sweet—O, hoo sweet! tho' whiles she had fears;

For a wee burdie sang, as roun' her it flew,
Sweet lassie, tak' tent—he's owre sweet to be true;
He's oot in the e'enin's whan ye dinna ken,
An' they say he's been seen wi' Kate o' the Glen.

But Effie wad lauch, an' wad sae to hersel',
What lees an' what clashes thae bodies maun tell,
For my Jamie has sworn to be true to the death,
An' nocht noo can pairt us as lang's we ha'e breath.

Ae short winter Sabbath, juist as it grew mirk,
The faither cam' hame—he had been at the kirk;
His cheek was sae white, an' his leuk was sae queer,
That Effie glower'd at him in dredour an' fear.

Then he said, "My ain Effie, puir mitherless lass!
Oh wha wad ha'e thocht this wad e'er come to pass?
Thy Jamie, this day, in the kirk was proclaim'd,
An' Katie MacLean for his bride they ha'e named.

I was tauld on the road by ane that maun ken,
Her grannie was ance the gudewife o' the Glen,
An' she left to young Katie a hantle o' gear—
It's gear Jamie wants, an' there's naething o't here."

N

An' what said puir Effie? She stood like a stane,
But faintin', or greetin', or cryin', was naue;
Her sweet lips they quiver'd, the bluid frae her cheek
Flew back to her heart, but nae word cou'd she speak.

The faither sat doun, laid her head on his breast:
"On God an' her faither my Effie maun rest,
They ne'er will deceive thee—thy wrangs are richt sair;
Gin Jamie had wed thee they micht ha'e been mair."

Sune Effie gat up, gied her faither some meat,
Put the bairnies to bed, yet ne'er could she greet—
Her young heart was stricken—the fountains were dry
That gush frae the een wi' a tearfu' supply.

That nicht at the reading she joined in the psalm,
Her cheek it was pale, but her brow it was calm;
An' faither he pray'd, as she knelt by his side,
That God his dear lassie wad comfort an' guide.

The winter gaed by, an' the hale simmer thro'
She tosh'd up the hoose, fed an' milkit the cow;
The cauld warl' had nocht that she cared for ava,
Her life it was silently meltin' awa'.

O! whaur noo the love-licht that sparkled ere while
In her bonny black e'e? O! whaur noo the smile
That dimpled her cheek? They were gane! they were
    gane!
Yet she ne'er shed a tear, an' ne'er made a mane.

An' sae she was wearin', fast wearin' awa'!
Wi' the leaves in October sweet Effie did fa'!
Her mournin' was ended, an' blissfu' an' bricht
The dear lassie dwells wi' the angels o' licht.

THE FATE OF MAXIMILIAN OF MEXICO AND HIS EMPRESS.

"TAKE physic, Pomp!" Look on that noble brow—
Of what avail thy garish splendours now—
The crown of Empire, worn for three short years,
Ending in madness, murder, blood, and tears?

Of stately form and mien, high-soul'd and brave—
From anarchy, misrule, and strife to save
He came. Deserted and deceived, he failed—
And fell, by twofold treachery assailed.

Unhappy Charlotte! Ah, the " weeping blood
In woman's heart" wells up into a flood
Of tender pity, while kind angels shed
Celestial tears on thy devoted head!

Oh, hapless victim, offered at the shrine
Of false ambition! more than death was thine,
When blank despair rung hope's expiring knell
Upon thine ear, till reason reeled and fell!

Allured to southern climes—oh, ill-starred pair!—
By hope's deluding meretricious glare—
An ignis fatuus, dazzling to betray,
Ye followed, fell, and perished in the way!

RHYMES FOR THE TIMES.—III.

AGAIN I ha'e ta'en to the clinkin' o' rhymes—
It's no on the signs, it's the deeds o' the times
O' whilk I wad speak; about what is gaun on
Aroun' us, amang us, an' farther beyon'.

Ye renegade churchmen, O ill be yer speed!
Ye've murdered auld Luther, an' stickit the creed;
Wi' Pusey for leader, ye'r marchin' on Rome,
Is "the wee bit endoomintie" yours whan ye come?

O spirit of Calvin! O shade of John Knox!
The Kirk is in danger, her faith orthodox;
In Moses, the God-given commandments an' law,
There are mony that say are worth naething ava.

Tho' whiles in the dark, this is clear at the least,
Oor rulers are giein' their power to the Beast;
I red them tak' tent, they may hear by-an'-by,
Frae millions o' men the "No Popery" cry.

Whan famishin' Tories, owre benches and stools,
Cam' loupin' an' yellin', the Whigamore fools
Left a' in their han's, an' took aff to the hill,
In the "Cave o' Adullam" was buried the bill.

Then Dizzy he stripp'd to the breeks an' the sark
To cleck a new Bill, it was unco warm wark,
Noo the puir thing's cleckit, an' oot o' the shell,
Belyve we sall see if it picks for itsel'.

O Sov'reign Victoria! bless'd and belov'd,
On the deck of the Albert thy mission was proved;
Thy han' grac'd the Sultan wi' garter and star,
And opened for freedom a pathway afar.

We're at peace wi' the warl', an' lang may it be,
In tradin' and fechtin' we're lords o' the sea;
But herry't wi' taxes, and rackit wi' toil,
By the lords o' the State, the mine, an' the soil.

O heavy the bluid o' the innocent hings
On the skirts o' vile hizzies: my auld heart it wrings
To hear that sae mony puir babies fin' death
At the mither's ain han', as sune's they draw breath.

Self-murder, an' a' kin' o' murders are rife,
Wife-beatin', garottin', and usin' the knife;
Abuses in unions are proved by the books,
The tin bombs an' bullets o' Broadhead an' Crookes.

The warst o' the ills that beset us, we think,
Is that curse o' the lan' the plague sore o' drink.
It poisons the sources an' streams o' oor life,
In youth an' in manhood, in mither an' wife.

We hae muckle that's ill, but mair that is gude;
Oor place 'mang the nations is weel understude—
Improvement in knowledge, in science, an' art—
The van of progression, oor post, an' oor part.

ADDRESS AND INVITATION

To a Young Friend who had gone over to Ireland in the interests
of his Political Party, at the Parliamentary Election of 1864.

To tell you the truth, dear J., I was sorry
To hear, by your note, that Whig, Roman, and Tory
Are taxing your patience, your time, and invention,
Not even the soft haunting voice that you mention
Has, by its sweet witchery, power to call back,
And make you rein up your political hack.
The deuce take the Tories; a fig for the Whigs;
A plague on the Romans and Radical prigs,
Who flounder and splash in the big Irish puddle,
Like geese in a bog, quack, gabble, and muddle;
Oh, botheration! such bustle and blarney—
I'd souse the whole herd in the Lakes of Killarney.
Too long, my dear J., on the shamrock you've trode,
Bedad they will dub you a son of the sod;
Come over, I bid you; come over the "say,"
We'll talk the thing out o'er a cup of good "tay."
Old grannie is waiting, to give you her hand,
The Rockingham's brimm'd, and the toast on the stand
Well brown'd and well butter'd;—the muse is com-
    plaining
That some wild Irish girl your heart is enchaining,

And vows, if you do not come back before long,
You'll never more quaff at the fountain of song.
Now this is an issue, for which you'll be sorry,
So come back—pray do—while the heather's in glory.

THE BLACK SNAKES.

"Look not upon the wine when it is red, when it giveth its colour in the cup, when it moveth itself aright. At the last it biteth like a serpent and stingeth like an adder."—Prov. xxiii. 31, 32.

A HAPPY child, a girl of ten,
    When autumn's golden tints were glowing,
And wilding fruits in brake and glen
    From nature's bounteous lap o'erflowing,

Went far into the tangled wild,
    Her little pail with luscious treasure
Of berries ripe to fill—the child
    Knew they would give her mother pleasure;

And still the little maid went on,
    And picked and gleaned till she grew weary;
She lost her way, the track was gone,
    And ah! the wood was lone and dreary.

The land was not a land like ours—
    From shingly mounds, and holes of hiding,
Leaving their trail on grass and flowers,
    Snakes, many-hued, were often gliding.

A freezing horror chilled my blood
    When first I heard what there befell her
Within that lone and darksome wood.
    Alas! the mother—who shall tell her?

The child ne'er saw her home again;
    And when the shades of eve were falling
The parents sought for her in vain,
    Their darling's name still wildly calling.

Kind neighbours came, the search was sped—
    In wood, in wild, in brake they sought her.
They sought in vain, till hope had fled—
    The child was dead, and so they thought her!

Six wintry months had come and gone,
    The earth was robed in summer glory;
And then to mourning friends was known
    The fearful sequel of my story.

Some youths who to the wilds had gone.
    Saw there a scene, the most appalling,
All o'er a spot they came upon
    Were many black snakes, twisting, crawling.

Close by—a thing of dread and fear—
    A little skeleton was lying.
They told the tale—soon far and near
    And all around the news went flying.

As white and smooth as ivory lay
   The bones, no speck of flesh remaining;
Devoured, ere it had felt decay,
   By swarming snakes, the young blood draining.

The parents of the missing child
   Came with the many thither flocking
To view the spot, far in the wild,
   Where acted was a scene so shocking.

A little pail, all rusted brown,
   Beside the small white bones was lying.
" My child, my child !"—it was her own—
   They heard the sobbing mother crying.

They fired the reptiles' hole, and then
   A hundred sable snakes came swarming
Out from the foul and fœtid den,
   A sight most hideous and alarming.

Sad mother, weeping for thy child,
   A woeful mother shares thy mourning
My son, too, strayed into the wild,
   I sought, but hope not, his returning.

Oh, early lost, my son, my son
   He strayed afar, in quest of pleasure ;
But found, ere he his quest had won,
   The serpent sting for promised treasure.

They told me, and I stood aghast,
  That on a spot where snakes were swarming,
A form, 'twas his, they found at last—
  A sight of horror, strange, alarming.

A skeleton, a ghastly heap
  Of naked bones, 'twas thus they found him ;
By snakes devoured in drunken sleep,
  The reptiles' holes yawned thickly round them.

Oh, ever open dens of death !
  Where life-devouring snakes are lurking,
Whose deadly bite and poisonous breath
  Inflame the curse for ever working.

Ah, pleasure-seeking youth ! beware
  The fiery curse your thousands dooming
To early death, disgrace, despair,
  The mind, the heart, the flesh consuming !

PAIRTIN' AN' MEETIN.'

O NANNIE, dear Nannie! whan ye gaed awa',
I thocht my fu' heart wad hae broken in twa;
An' sair ye were sabbin', tho' close by yer side
Stood the true lovin' lad wha made ye his bride.

Thro' the green wuds o' Murdiestane, O! never mair
Bareheidit, barefitit, wi' win'-touzled hair,
A' pechin', an' blawin', an' lauchin', we'll rin
Till the shadows fa' doun, an' gloamin' sets in.

The corn-craik was chirmin' her lane eerie cry,
Whan aff we gaed skelpin' to ca' hame the kye;
An' up the green gill, as we drave them alang,
We rous'd a' the echoes wi' daffin' an' sang.

But Nannie, dear lassie, was sune a young wife,
An' listed to fecht the stern battle o' life;
In the bonny green gill we'll sing never mair—
We pairted, an' wow but oor pairtin' was sair.

The muircock was crawin', the dew on the corn,
The laverock singin' that sweet July morn,
Whan Nannie an' Jamie stapp'd owre the door-stane—
'Twas waesome to see hoo their pairtin' was ta'en.

Auld Johnnie, the faither, wi' pow like the snaw,
Held her haun as he ne'er cou'd ha'e let it awa';
The mither was sabbin' an' claspin' her neck,
An' kiss'd her dear Nannie wi' heart like to break.

Then Jamie, whase true heart was swallin' fu' big,
Said, " Ye maun come wi' us a bit doun the rig;
Whan awa', wi' gude health, fu' brawly we'll fen',
An' aft o' oor weelfare we'll gi'e ye to ken."

He pu'd a sweet bab o' the red heather bells :
" For love o' auld Scotlan' we'll share't 'mang oorsel's
Keep that in remembrance o' them that's awa',
An' this sall gae wi' us whate'er be oor fa'."

The faither richt reverently barein' his head,
His een fu' o' tears, an' his twa hauns ootspread,
Socht the blessin' o' God, the licht o' His face,
To gang wi' his bairns to their far-awa' place.

An' sune the young twasome sailed aff to the west,
An' there, 'mang the Yankees, they teuk up their rest ;
By water an' fire they were herrit and spoil'd
O' ilk thing they had, still they hoped an' they toil'd.

Whan the auld folk at hame o' this had heard tell,
It strack on their he'rts wi' a sorrowfu' knell ;
The mither sabb'd oot, " I sall never ha'e rest
Till I clasp my dear bairn again to my breast."

Quo' Johnnie, " Gudewife, the neist month I'm four-
    score ;
We've a hogger weel filled, an' claith in gude store ;
Ye ha'e sheets, ye ha'e blankets, an' coverin's braw,
An' oor ae bonny bairn maun noo get them a'."

They sauld aff their stock, an' pack'd up their gear ;
Oot owre the Atlantic they boun' them to steer :
On Scotlan' the bodies ha'e leukit their last,
An' safe to the new frae the aul' warl' pass'd.

I spake o' their pairtin'; but words mayna speak
O' their meetin' again—hoo Nannie's pale cheek,
A' dreepin' wi' tears, to the mither's was press'd,
And Johnnie ance mair held his bairn to his breast.

Then in time we heard tell that, far in the west,
The foursome were settled in comfort an' rest ;
There the young had a hame, the auld folk a grave,
Owre whilk the dark locust an' red maple wave.

THE MIDNIGHT VIGIL.

MOURNFUL, sighing, sadly weeping,
Sleepless 'midst a household sleeping;
Midnight's lonely vigil keeping,
 Darkling and alone;
From my sore each friend and lover
Stand aloof, I may not cover
The burning wound that all discover—
 Comforters are none.

Rachel for her children wailing
With a woe how unavailing
Aught to soothe—and comfort failing
 To assuage her moans.
The Jewish mother, Ramah's daughter,
When her babes were given to slaughter,
Saw their pure young blood like water
 Pour'd upon the stones.

'Midst her martyred infants kneeling,
High the wail of anguished feeling,
Mother's love, and woe revealing,
 Thrilled upon the air;
Then were seen bright angels bending
O'er the slain—white wings extending
To waft the spirits heavenward tending—
 She has found them there.

o

But, ah ! the children of my sorrow—
Night is theirs—no hopeful morrow :
Alas ! worn heart, where wilt thou borrow
    Words thy grief to show ?
Oh, my sons, ere sin beguiling
Plunged you into depths defiling
Of intemperance, treacherous smiling—
    Gulf of sin and woe !

Ye were innocent and loving,
Mother's deepest yearnings moving,
Her soft arms and bosom proving
    Shelter still and rest.
Babes of Bethlehem, loved and cherished,
Would my babes like you had perished !
Reft while sinless, spotless, cherished,
    From the mother's breast.

They were spared, were fostered, nourished,
Plants of hope, they bloomed and flourished,
Yet they withered, fell and perished,
    In their summer prime.
Lost, oh lost ! Say not for ever,
One there is who can deliver,
Seek and save the lost—dissever
    Youth from guilt and crime.

WELCOME TO OCTOBER, 1867.

I HAIL and bless thy presence, month most dear
In the round cycle of the rolling year ;
Thy grave, sweet aspect, silent and serene,
Is dearer now than it hath ever been.
When brooding sorrows shroud my soul in gloom,
And round me fall the shadows of the tomb,
Thy mellow radiance, tender and benign,
Softly irradiates this sad heart of mine.
For ah ! my way of life has fallen now
Into the sere and yellow leaf; but thou,
Most beauteous in decay, to me dost bring
A deeper bliss than all the flush of Spring.
How sweet the sympathetic chord that thrills
My musing soul, when o'er the purple hills
I see the mantling mists creep slowly down,
While from the forest monarch's leafy crown
The gems are falling, and the shining threads
Of gossamer thick strung with dewy beads.
From the blue depths of yon calm sleeping sky,
Spirit of Peace, thou com'st; I feel thee nigh:
O, on my soul's dark waters gently move,
As at creation's birth the brooding dove !
And I, oh gentle peace, will muse and sing
In the soft shadow of thy downy wing.

Spring with her clouds, her sunbursts, and her
    showers,
Bright glowing Summer, draped and crowned with
    flowers,
Ripe Autumn, rich in fruits and golden sheaves,
Have pass'd away like swallows from the eaves:
But thou, October, with thy sober hues,
Thy russet foliage, and thy drenching dews,
Thy silent songsters, blanch'd and faded flowers,
Canst with soft magic charm life's weary hours.

PICTURES OF MEMORY.

I.

A SMALL thatched cottage, moss grown old,
   A low-browed, weather-beaten door,
Two windows small, that dimly light
   The dusky walls and earthen floor.

From rafters, grimed with smoke and eld,
   Hang bunch'd-up herbs, a triple row,
Shedding their strongly-scented breath
   Through all the dingy room below.

Beside the southern casement sings,
   Within his cage, a linnet grey;
Beneath, upon the window-seat,
   A pot with flowering lupines gay.

A matron plies her spinning wheel;
   With dancing feet, her little daughter
Trips to her side; her dark brown eyes
   And dimpled cheeks are bright with laughter.

In fairy tales and ballad lore
   The little maid had wondrous pleasure;
The tiny volume in her hand,
   The last addition to her treasure.

With grave, kind look the mother gazed
    Into her darling's beaming eyes :—
" My child such reading may amuse,
    But will not make you good and wise."

" Oh, you shall hear," the child replies :
    Then warbled clear an old Scotch ditty.
The mother's heart was moved ; her eyes
    Were brimming o'er with love and pity.

She smiled, and softly laid her hand
    Upon the fair child's shining hair,
Who, like a dancing sunbeam, pass'd
    Away into the summer air.

II.

A little, lowly, flowery dell,
A sylvan nook, where fays may dwell—
In purple fairy thimbles hiding,
Till the moon in heaven is gliding ;
And the silver runnel, glancing,
'Neath her beams is softly dancing—
Still dancing, to its own sweet tune,
Beneath the midnight sky of June.
Opening from the fairy dell,
How sweet the scene, and soft the spell

That Nature, in her blandest mood,
Has spread o'er this blest solitude!
Cushions, soft, of richest moss,
Of emerald hue, and velvet gloss,
And wilding briers, ablush with roses,
At every turn the path encloses;
While, drooping from the mossy trees—
Pouring rich nectar for the bees
From every honey-scented cell—
The eglantine perfumes the dell;
In richest purple bloom, a bed
Of fragrant mountain thyme is spread.
I pause to drink the odours sweet,
Crushed out beneath my careless feet.

GRANNIE'S DREAM.

A TRUE INCIDENT.

BESIDE the winter e'ening fire,
    A gleg wee lass o' towmonds ten,
Sat nestlin' close to Grannie's knee,
    Upon the cozie clean fire-en'.

The mither, croonin' ower a sang,
    Sat spinning in the ingle neuk,
An' aften on the twasume she
    Wad cast a couthie, kin'ly leuk.

In cowl and bauchles faither sat,
    Aft nodding in his muckle chair;
The supper sowens stood on the bink—
    A supper whilk a queen micht share.

Wi' pawkie e'e, the farrant bairn
    Keek'd up in Grannie's face, and said,
" O, ye maun min' the promise noo
    That but yestreen to me ye made.

" I heard ye say maist feck o' dreams
　　Were nocht but nonsense, yet it seems
That aften warnin's gude and true
　　Are sent us frae the lan' o' dreams.

" An' noo ye'll tell me, Grannie dear,
　　Some dreams that ye hae had yersel',
That afterhen ye ne'er forgat,
　　An' proven true by what befell."

The croonin' sang, the birrin' wheel,
　　Had stoppit baith ; the mither raise
An' brocht some peats to beet the fire,
　　An' syne sat doun to warm her taes.

" Noo tent me, lassie," Grannie said,
　　" I was a gilpie like thysel',
Whan sic a dream ae nicht I had
　　That aye it grues my heart to tell.

" I thocht no ane was in the house,
　　That by the fire alane I sat,
Had in my haun a water jug,
　　An' at my feet the auld grey cat.

" The beast sprang up wi' glow'rin' e'en,
　　An' ran to hide the bed beneath,
I leukit doun an' there I saw
　　What I sall min' while I hae breath.

" A muckle haun, nocht but a haun,
　Was lyin' on the floor outspread ;
A haun as big as ony ten,
　The colour o't a bluidy red.

" I had nae fear, but lichtly lauch'd,
　An' at the haun I flang the jug ;
O never till the 'crack o' doom'
　Will fa' sic soun' on mortal lug.

" A soun', mair loud than thunner far,
　Rang through the air, aroun', abroad ;
An' whan it ceas'd, an awfu' voice
　Bade me prepare to meet my God.

" The wee short hour ayont the twal,
　Frae oot the clock that moment rung ;
I wauken't wi' a fearfu' skreigh,
　An' fast to mither's neck I clung.

" I tauld to her my dream.　She said,
　' Noo frae thy dream this lesson learn,
Ne'er to despise the haun o' God,
　Or cast contempt on it, my bairn.

" An' if thou come to woman's years,
　An' aye through life hast meekly trod
In wisdom's ways, thou'lt be prepared
　Whan soun's the ca' to meet thy God.'

" It's threescore years sinsyne, yet aft
  Comes to my min' that dream sae clear ;
The haun I see, the soun,' the voice,
  The awsume words I seem to hear.

" Whan in the howe o' nicht I hear
  The clock ring oot her single knell,
' Prepare to meet thy God ' it seems
  To say—how soon we canna tell.

" An' noo, my bairn, my dream is tauld,
  I houp that it may bring thee gude ;
That dream a blessin' was to me,
  Though at the first ill unnerstude."

" O Grannie," said the frichtit bairn—
  Her cheek was white, her dark broun e'e
Was fu' o' tears—" I'll ne'er forget
  The dream ye tauld this nicht to me."

TO MITHERS.

HEAR me, mithers, oh ! mithers,
  Wives o' puir workin' men,
Wha toil baith late an' early—
  Little to spare or spen';
Weel ken I, my titties,
  Hoo ye maun haud an' hain,
Tentily warein' the gear
  That feeds an' cleeds your ain.

Sair the gudeman is needin'
  New claes to fend the cauld—
New shoon that may turn the weet
  That's seepin' through the auld.
Bairnies are roun' ye hingin',
  Milk an' meal they maun hae,
Frocks an' knickers forbye—
  A' maun come aff the pay.

The bairnies maun get schulin',
   An' though the fees be sma',
Mony wees mak' a muckle;
   Hoo sall ye compass a'?
Nocht but a stout-heart mither
   Can climb sae stey a brae;
Dinna weary in weel-doin'—
   Whaur there's a will there's a way.

Dinna stan' lang at the door,
   For gossips will come oot,
Tellin' an' speerin' the news,
   Ca'in' the clashes aboot.
Bide maist on your ain fire en',
   The bairnies roun' your knee,
Learnin' the fear o' Gude:
   Be what a mither shou'd be.

Kaim weel the towzie wee heids,
   Wash the wee faces an' feet:
Makin' an' mendin' their duds,
   Try to gar baith ends meet.
Mind ye to tosh up the hoose
   Before the gudeman comes in;
Set doun his meals wi' a smile—
   Ne'er wi' flytin' an' din.

Mithers, I've something to say :
    Sairly it grieves me to think
Monie among ye are gaun
    Clean to the deil wi' drink ;
Keepin' the hoose like a midden,
    Bairnies hunger't an' wan,
Fleein' wi' rags, barkin't wi' dirt :
    Wae for the workin' man !

There's nae sic plague on the yirth,
    There's nae sic curse in life,
Like the curse that blichts the hame
    That hauds a drucken wife.

LINES

ON THE DEATH OF THE INFANT DAUGHTER OF DAVID YOUNG,
DUNOON.

O EARLY snowdrop, pure and pale!
Could mother's love and tears avail,
The drooping bells would still have spread
Their snowy petals on the bed—
That bed of love the mother's breast—
The tender flow'ret's dearest rest.
Sweet baby snowdrop! short thy rest
On the fond mother's loving breast,
For ah! too soon, the icy grasp
Of death unloosed the tender clasp
That sheltered from the winter storm
The tiny flow'ret's fading form.
Pale babe! thy earthly robe of white
Is fallen now.   In robes of light
Arrayed! a baby angel thou:
The Father's seal upon thy brow,
For near His throne He gives thee place,
And evermore behold His face.

The yearning love, the tender smile
That lit the parents' eyes, the while,
The little while, their flower was given,
To bud on earth, and bloom in heaven.
Sweet flower! the chilling blasts of time
Invade not that celestial clime,
Where, basking in the Father's smile,
Thou wait'st the dear ones left erewhile.

MEDLEY OF THOUGHTS AND FEELINGS
ON THE ITALIAN CRISIS.

"HAD I a thousand mouths, a thousand tongues,
A thousand throats, inspired with brazen lungs,"
I'd rouse with thunder tones the slumbering world,
Till Pope, and priest, and Papacy be hurl'd
Down from their gilded thrones.   The exulting earth
Would hail with loud acclaim the glorious birth
Of truth celestial, freedom, light, and love,
Goodwill to man, and peace with heaven above.

Seek ye for liberty ?—shall she be found
Where soul, and heart and conscience all are bound ?
Where sinful man before a sinner kneels,
To him his thoughts, his very heart reveals
What he has done, is doing ; seeks to find
Full absolution ?   Blind, oh bound and blind !

"Woman, what think'st thou of thy husband now?"
Said one, who bore on his Satanic brow
The stain of martyr's blood.   Replied the wife,
"I ever thought much of him when in life,
But ne'er so much as now, when on the heath,
Bathed in his martyr blood, he lies in death."

P

Dark ruler of the Gaul, so sayest thou,
" What thinks Italia of her hero now ?"
The captive rebel, he who dared to cope
With Gallic legions, sent by France to prop
Old John, the Jesuit's frail crumbling throne ;
Just going, going, going—must be gone.

She loves him more than in his noon of life,
When, daring tyranny to mortal strife,
" He came, he saw, he conquered," freely gave
The kingdoms he had won— O true and brave !
To him he gave them who now stands aloof—
Of kingly gratitude a pregnant proof.

And we too love him with a love so deep
It bleeds, it burns, but cannot stoop to weep
For him, for him who lies in captive thrall.
Oh bitter draught, the wormwood and the gall,
When drained at the behest of such as thou,
With freedom's life-blood on thy branded brow !

God save thee, Garibaldi ! for the hour
That soon will strike the knell of Papal power
And Gallic intervention ; and a home
For truth and liberty be found in Rome.

FREEDOM FOR ITALY—1867.

" HE is the freeman whom the Truth makes free;
All else are slaves," I cry aloud to thee,
O Garibaldi ! in the fateful hour.
Think not 'tis in mere human might or power,
Not even the might of such an arm as thine,
To compass freedom, lasting, true, divine—
Not the keen edge of thy all-conquering sword
Can cut the Gordian double-knotted cord
That ignorance and superstition winds
With deadening strain round captive human minds.
Slaves of the Papacy ! when will ye know
That, to be free, yourselves must strike the blow ?
Your souls are shackled, and your hearts benumbed,
And even majestic Reason has succumbed,
And, stumbling in the gloom of Papal night,
Moves blindfold, still eschewing truth and light.
Awake ! ye sleepers in the dust ! Awake !
For truth, for freedom, for your country's sake !
Awake from your enchanted sleep ! Arise !
Shake off the accursed spell ; unclose your eyes.
The Word of Life, the Sun of Truth has risen ;
To read, to hear insures not now a prison.
No more Madais in dungeon cells immured
By priests intolerant.   Ye are secured

From wrongs like these.   To every hearth and home
The Word of God may safely, freely come;
And he who runs may read, if read he can,
How God gives freedom to enslavèd man.
True patriots! say if ye have ever found
That men were free where truth was gagg'd and bound?
Sacred and social liberty must be
Conjoined ere Italy be truly free.
Small glory yours in conflict with the Pope;
'Tis with the Papacy that ye must cope,
And not with flesh and blood; a sterner war,
More dark, more dread, more difficult by far,
The conquest of the erring, human soul,
Subdued, subjected long to its control.
The two-edged sword, the Word of God, to wield,
Be yours in combat on this battle-field;
Diffuse the truth, give all the power to read:
" They whom the truth makes free are free indeed."

Great chieftain! hero of a hundred fights!
What is the fame that most thy soul delights?—
Italian union, liberty, and Rome
Her capital in all time yet to come?
God grant thy heart's desire, thy wish fulfil,
Perhaps not now, but when and how He will!

GRANNIE'S CRACK ABOOT THE FAMINE IN AULD SCOTLAN' IN 1739-40.

"Oh saw ye e'er sic witless bairns,
    Sic wasterie o' blessin's gien?
Oh had they dree'd what we ha'e dree'd,
    Oh had they seen what we ha'e seen!

"See hoo they break the gude ait-cake,
    An' spit the moolins oot their mou';
They're lucky fu', an' lucky het,
    An' lucky near the mill, I trow."

Sae spak' my gutcher, roun' his chair
    His ain gran' bairns were makin' fun,
Aft tedding frae their careless hauns
    Their bits o' pieces on the grun'.

"Gude bless the bairns," my grannie said,
    Syne, turnin' frae her spinning wheel,
She drew her creepie near the fire—
    "I ken, gudeman, ye lo'e them weel.

"Sair was the dool that we hae dree'd,
    An' sair the sights that we hae seen,
But we hae been preserved through a'—
    Praise to His blessed name be gi'en!

"That waefu' year I'll ne'er forget,
　　Ay, though it's unco lang sinsyne;
That year ye'll min' fu' weel yersel',
　　The seventeen hunner thretty-nine.

"The craps had fail'd for towmonds twa;
　　The meal was dear, an' next to nane
For luve or siller cou'd ye get,
　　Tho' owre braid Scotlan' ye had gane.

"Auld Scotlan' owre her thistle grat—
　　Noo that her mutchkin stoup was dry—
For meal pocks toom, an' aumries bare,
　　An' starvin' bairnie's waefu' cry.

"The frost lay a' that winter thro';
　　The yird was hard as ony stane;
An' famine to the cottars cam',
　　An' crined them doun to skin an' bane.

"My faither's girnel wasna toom;
　　We aye had something to the fore;
But oh! the starvin' wives an' bairns
　　That aften wannert roun' the door!

"The milky syn'ings o' the kirn,
　　The scartin's o' the parritch pat,
The bairns wad lick frae 'tween the stanes,
　　As they upon their groufs lay flat.

" An' turnip taps, an' green kail blades,
　　Were gather't up, an' carried hame—
Whan boil'd, the mithers were richt glad
　　Wi' sic like things to fill their wame.

" The spring was dreigh, and bitter cauld,
　　The trees were lang ere they were clad,
The wonner was hoo puir folk leeve't,
　　An' hoo their bairns were warm'd an' fed.

" Ae day I wanner't to the wud,
　　An' gather't sticks the fire to beet;
An' there an unco sicht I saw,
　　That made me baith to glow'r an' greet.

" I'se warran there were hauf-a-score
　　O' hunger-stricken wives an' weans,
Thrang pu'in' frae the bare dyke side
　　Young nettles, spite o' stingin' pains.

" An' branches o' the beech wi' leaves
　　But hauflins spread, they stripped bare,
I saw them eat the leaves wi' greed,
　　An' gi'e them to their weanies there.

" An' aft, whan naither bite nor sowp
　　The parents could their bairnies gie,
They wad contrive some slee bit ploy
　　To stap their cravin's for a wee.

" My faither's neebor, Robin Steel—
    His wife an' him ye'll min', gudeman?—
Ae nicht their bairns were greetin' sair,
    Till Robin thocht him o' a plan.

" A wecht he fill'd wi' dry peat ase
    Amang the whilk some pease he mix'd—
In that the bairns wad graip and wale,
    Till sleep their weary een had fix'd.

" The cottar faither, weak wi' want,
    Wad stacher to the farmer's ha',
A scone or twa the wife wad gie,
    If she had ocht to spare ava.

" Then tears ran doun his pykit cheeks,
    And he wad thank her wi' his een,
But ne'er a bit o't cross'd his craig
    Till it was dealt at hame, I ween.

" Oh mony a bairn fell frae the breast,
    An' lay upon the mither's knee
Like some wee wallow't lily flouir,
    Till death would kin'ly close its e'e.

" An' mony a puir auld man and wife
    That winter dee't wi' want an cauld ;
They couldna beg, and sae their need
    To neebors puir was never tauld.

" Oor Scottish puir had aye some pride—
   An' honest, decent pride, I ween ;
Sair want an' sufferin' they thol't
   Ere they wad let their need be seen.

" That randy quean, Job's graceless wife,
   Wha bade him curse his God and dee—
Auld Scotlan' wad hae cuff'd her lugs
   Had she been here advice to gie.

" Yet there was mony a stricken heart,
   Whase faith an' hope was like to fail ;
But aye some word in season cam'
   To mak' the wounded speerit hale.

" An' ye micht hear, baith e'en an' morn,
   In mony a hame, the voice o' prayer,
Though ne'er a peat to beet the fire,
   Or bread to fill the mou' was there.

" Ae day, I slipp'd my parritch cog
   A'neath my jupe, an' ran wi' speed
To Robin Steel's, for sair I fear'd
   That they had naither meal nor bread.

" The mither took it in her haun'
   And liftit up to Heaven her e'e,
An' thankit God for what was gi'en,
   Ere she wad let the bairnies pree.

"That mither—ay, and mony mair
   That thro' the fiery trials pass'd—
Like silver seven times purified,
   Cam' oot the furnace pure at last.

"An' noo, gudeman, I'll haud my tongue,
   I needna noo sae muckle mair;
But pray that Scotlan' ne'er again
   May see sic times—sae sad an' sair."

BE HOPEFUL.

I.

THE LARK.

Morning is doffing her mantle of grey ;
Up from·the sod to the portals of day
The blithe lark is soaring—carolling free,
Musical spirit o'erflowing with glee.

Storm clouds may darken the fair brow of spring,
Hush the sweet songster and ruffle his wing ;
When the bright sunshine comes after the rain,
The lark is soaring and singing again.

Buoyantly, brightly, in life's sunny morn,
Child of the Muses, we saw thee upborne,
Spreading thy pinions the white clouds among,
Pouring thy thrilling and rapturous song.

Thy song may be hushed, thy plumage be soiled,
Struck from the summit to which thou hast toiled :
Be hopeful, thy pinions may bear thee again
On high, and thy song be poured not in vain.

II.

THE ROSE.

Blushing and glowing, the rose in full bloom,
Jewell'd with dewdrops and rich in perfume;
Fairest of blossoms, a gem and a joy,
Her charms never pall, her sweets never cloy.

Remembrance may fade in sorrow and strife,
The darkness, the storms, the winter of life;
Summer returning will bring in her train
The rose in her bloom and fragrance again.

See the sweet rosebud her petals unfold!
The gems on her breast of value untold;
The dewdrop, the ruby, the lustrous pearl,
Meet emblems of thee, pure, innocent girl.

The trail of the snake is over thy name,
Dimm'd are thy gems, and sullied thy fame:
Virtue will triumph, detraction will die,
The rose and the gem smile up to the sky.

III.

THE STREAM.

A bright stream may shrink in summer's hot fire,
Flowers on her margin may droop and expire;
Her channel be dry, her soft gushing tone,
The voice of the stream be silent and gone.

Lost nymph of the stream, we find thee again;
Clouds from their treasures have pour'd out the rain;
Thy channel is full, thou glidest along,
Flowers on thy margin and mirth in thy song.

Brightly and swiftly, with laughter and song,
The life-stream of youth runs sparkling along;
Oft on the margin, enamelled with flowers,
Youth in wild pleasure is wasting the hours.

Fierce fires of passion are scorching his veins,
The bright stream hath shrunk 'neath horrors and pains;
God speaks in thunder—the rain-torrent pours—
The life-stream again runs fresh 'mong the flowers.

IV.

THE RESUMÉ.

Be hopeful, sweet singer; man may not raise
To lays that thou pourest high peans of praise:
The nightingale's song will ever delight,
Though sung in the gloom and silence of night.

Beautiful maiden, may never envy
Blanch thy sweet roses and dim thy bright eye:
Purity, innocence, God is thy guide,
Angels shall guard and watch by thy side.

Bright stream, we bless thee ; we trace thee afar
Down the green valley ; Hope's beautiful star
Gleams on thy bosom ; may never again
Wild fires of passion thy life-current drain.

Be hopeful, hope ever ; hope never dies ;
In midst of our sorrows hope ever lies :
The hot brow of anguish, cooled by the balm
Dropp'd from her pinions, is trustful and calm.

THE DYING OLD YEAR, 1867.

"Avaunt, away! dread shapes of hate and fear
That hover round me," moan'd the dying Year:
"Dark treason, superstition, and misrule!
Man, 'neath your sway, is victim, dupe, or tool.
I know ye, whence ye are: back, demons, fly
To native darkness: leave me peace to die.
What sounds appalling stun my dying ear—
Explosive, crashing, cries of pain and fear!
Rebellion, murder, flout the face of day,
And stalk abroad in long and grim array.
Ye men in power, must ye be men of straw?
Arise, assert the majesty of law!
Stern justice, rule, and order—these maintain:
Ye bear the sword, then bear it not in vain.
Protect good men and true: the lawless curb:
Must traitors ever thus your peace disturb?
I die. Yet hear my words before I go:
Arrest the traitorous current in its flow;
Roll back the Papal tide that comes, is come,
Has spread, is spreading o'er your island home."

He ceased awhile and feebly gasp'd for breath:
Then faintly muttered, "Hark, the voice of death—

He comes, he comes, in league with demon war,
The thunder of his wheels I hear from far !
My eyes are dark—oh see you not the cloud
That veils broad Europe's sky as with a shroud?
Gallic warriors guard Rome's sovereign priest,
And vultures on Italia's heroes feast ;
On red Mentana fell her youthful braves,
And Freedom weeps upon their bloody graves.

" My hours are numbered ; midnight rings my knell ;
Friends of my youth, eternally farewell !
My young successor on the threshold stands—
Oh, greet him well, with open hearts and hands ;
May brighter auguries and happier times
Be his !   Ring out the happy New Year chimes.
I go," he murmur'd low, " I faint, I die,"
Then passed away, with one low, moaning sigh.

A BALLAD,

FOUNDED ON A REAL INCIDENT WHICH OCCURRED IN HIGH LIFE,
MANY YEARS AGO.

WITHIN a princely chamber sat
  A lady, not alone;
Her queenly brow, so white and high,
  No shadow lay upon.

Her slender fingers lightly press'd
  The jewel, bright and rare,
That on her heaving bosom gleam'd—
  Her lord had placed it there.

"There let it rest, my peerless one,"
  Her noble husband said;
" And take the lustrous pearls I bring,
  Thy raven hair to braid.

"Come, I will lead thee to a scene
  In my ancestral halls,
Where genius, art, and beauty shine
  Upon the pictured walls.

" There many a form of grace and love
  The painter's hand hath thrown
Upon the canvas—form like thine
  His art hath never shown."

Q

The palace gallery was rich
    In paintings rare and old;
With sculptured marbles ranged between,
    Of value all untold.

And all along that gallery fair,
    They wandered side by side—
She gazing on the paintings rare,
    He on his beauteous bride.

Oft through the garden walks they strayed,
    Amid the flush of flowers;
Or sat with claspèd hands beneath
    The lovely Eden bowers.

And when she rode, or walked, she found
    Him ever by her side;
On "angel wings" that happy year
    The moments seem'd to glide.

" I go, my love, but with thy leave,
    To try my racer's speed
Upon the course—a noble Earl
    And I have so agreed."

"Then go, my love," she smiling said,
    "Thy will is ever mine;
From friends and pleasures I would not
    Thee ever thus confine."

He rode afar into the west;
   And when he came again,
" I fear," he said, " my own beloved,
   My stay hath caused thee pain."

She smiled; he took her in his arms,
   And pressed her to his breast;
" How could I go, how could I stay,
   Of love like thine possess'd ?"

Oh, serpent, hid among the leaves
   Of love's most fragrant flower,
Thou now has left thy trail within
   Thy lady's stainless bower.

And oft she saw him go and come ;
   But though she inly pined,
Suspicion of his broken vows
   Ne'er touched her generous mind.

She in her princely chamber sat ;
   But now she sat alone ;
Her queenly brow, so white and pure,
   A shadow lay upon.

" Go thou, my maid," she said, " and bring
   The pot of soft perfume
With which I wont to dress my hair,
   'Tis in his lordship's room."

The maiden went, an open note
   Within the drawer lay—
She saw, she knew the name below,
   A lady light and gay.

She gave it to her lady's hand ;
   "And oh ! forgive," she said,
"If I am wrong—alas ! I fear
   Thou foully art betrayed."

And when she read the fatal note,
   Her cheek grew cold and pale ;
Yet, noble heart and lofty soul,
   Would neither yield nor quail.

Full proof the cruel missive gave
   Of what had passed between
The guilty pair ; and named a place
   Where they might meet unseen.

She from her finger tore the ring,
   The jewel from her breast,
The pearls from her hair, and firm
   Her foot upon them press'd.

Then picked the shining fragments up,
   And cast them on the flame ;
"I ne'er shall look on him again,
   Or bear his hated name.

" Go, maiden, tell my servant true
   To take my carriage round
Behind the wood—by dawn of day
   I will not here be found."

Then down the marble stairs she stole ;
   The night was still and dark ;
And leaning on her maiden's arm,
   They sped across the park.

They found the carriage, stepp'd within,
   And swiftly drove away ;
The lordly towers were far behind
   At dawning of the day.

Four nights and days they posted on,
   And only stopp'd to bait
And rest the horses—longer time
   The lady would not wait.

" To England—to my father's halls :
   Thank God, no blood of thine,
Thou recreant false, shall mingle with
   My father's spotless line."

Surprise and wonder, scorn and ire,
   Flushed on the father's face
At what he heard ; he clasped his child
   In loving, long embrace.

"Go to thy mother's room; for she
  Will take thee to her heart,
And from her loving arms no more
  Her darling will depart."

But what of him, that lord so false?
  Next day, at twilight hour,
He came, and soon went up to see
  His lady in her bower.

He softly knock'd and gently call'd,
  But answer there was none;
He ask'd her page if that he knew
  His lady forth had gone.

" I know not, O, my lord," he said—
  "She was not seen to-day,
And none within the palace saw
  My lady go away."

Again he softly knock'd and call'd,
  But still no answer came;
All night he watched beside the door,
  Still calling on her name.

Then they unlock'd the chamber door,
  And in he wildly rushed;
The rooms, the bed, were empty—all
  In deadly silence hush'd.

He search'd the chamber o'er and found,
  Upon the window seat,
A note that made his bold eye quail,
  And guilty bosom beat.

His lady's hand the note inscrib'd;
  But when he looked within,
He only found the fatal note,
  That told his shame and sin.

What need we say?—he saw, he felt,
  The guilty secret love
The note revealed, had scared to flight
  His pure and faithful dove.

The beautous star, whose light benign
  His palace halls illum'd,
Will shine no more upon a name
  By truth and honour doom'd.

The holy bands that bound their hands,
  Stern law came in to sever;
The star that shone on life's young dream,
  For him is set for ever.

DULEEP SINGH,

AN INDIAN PRINCE NOW RESIDENT IN ENGLAND.

OF late I listened to a wondrous tale
　From lips revered.　'Twas not of war and glory—
A moving tale of princely love and truth,
　Quite a new version of the " old, old story."

From India's golden, glowing, sunny clime,
　A youthful prince to favoured England came,
And found the Light of Life—the life that sheds
　Divinest glory on the Saviour's name !

Victoria, pattern of all virtues rare—
　The good, the wise, the tender and benign—
With tender sympathy, and welcome fair,
　Received this stranger youth of princely line.

O happy Prince ! The diamond, " Mount of Light "—
　The treasured gem, whose lambent glories shone
Like clustered stars—he lost ; but found instead
　The Pearl of Price ! nor mourned the diamond gone.

Led by a hand divine, to Cairo old
　He went.　And lo ! a vision of delight
Rose like a star on his admiring eyes :
　A fair young maiden—pious, pure, and bright !

Meek child of Providence, true child of grace,
   Beloved, devoted teacher of the young !
Ah ! never stranger tale of love than thine,
   Sweet " Bamba," has the raptured poet sung.

Love at first sight, with gentle violence, stormed
   The Prince's heart.   He yielded to its power,
He sought and won the timid maid, who had
   But beauty, love, and goodness for her dower.

When first his eyes fell on that youthful form,
   A secret voice—intuitive, divine—
Said to his heart, Behold this gentle maid ;—
   The heart replied, She shall, she must be mine.

And soon her young and tender heart was given
   Into his keeping ; soon the small soft hand
Was joined to his ; the mission'd man of God
   Bound them, with joy, in holy wedlock's band.

In Cairo's mission-home the Prince had found
   The precious gem he on his bosom wore :
His own in life, in death, in weal and woe—
   To sparkle, love, and bless him evermore.

Rich was the golden gift the fair young bride,
   Sent by her princely husband, came to lay
Upon the Mission altar.   God, she said,
   Had, as her Father, given His child away ;—

Giv'n her to him, who led her to a home—
  A happy English home, by love made bright.
One Lord, one faith was theirs—one hope that shines
  And sheds on all Heaven's pure, supernal light.

And when a baby boy, to crown and bliss
  Their wedded love, to their embrace was given,
Our gracious Queen, as sponsor at the font,
  Gave the dear babe, in holy rite, to Heaven.

There, too, the Sovereign lady gave the name
  Of "Albert Victor" to the infant boy :—
The worth such names imply be his in life—
  A life of goodness, purity, and joy !

THE FEAST OF THE "MUTCHES."

[VERSES COMMEMORATIVE OF THE ANNUAL SUPPER GIVEN TO POOR OLD
WOMEN, IN THE CITY HALL, GLASGOW, ON JANUARY 3, 1868, WHEN
NEARLY TWO THOUSAND WERE PRESENT, ALL WEARING WHITE
"MUTCHES."]

I'M a lamiter, Girzie, or I wad hae been
At the feast o' the mutches hauden yestreen
In the big City Ha'—the notion was gran':
Thanks to the gude bodies wha thocht o' the plan.

A thoosan' white mutches !—what think ye o' that ?
Nae haffitless bannet, nae bloomer or hat,
Was worn by the grannies that nicht in the ha',
Juist snod pipet mutches as white as the snaw.

We've a' heard tell o' " Rab Rorison's bannet.
It wasna' the bannet, the heid that was in it "—
In that lay its value ; the same thing, I trow,
Is said o' the mutches we speak aboot noo.

That heid is as white as the mutch that it wears,
An' aft it's been like to a fountain o' tears,
Aye gushin' and tricklin' doun frae the een—
A puir lanely bodie, wi' few to befrien'.

An' see, there's anither, that aye in the strife,
The dolour an' din in the battle o' life,
Though burnin' an' gowpin wi' sorrow an' pain,
An' bow'd to the yirth, wad rise hopefu' again.

There's ane wi' a face that ne'er glunches nor girns,
Though she wins her bit bread by fillin' o' pirns;
She never was wed, keepit clear o' the men,
A canny auld maiden, o' threescore an' ten.

An' there's a puir heid that's been cutit and clour'd,
But Heaven an' hersel' kens what she endured
Lang years frae a drucken ill-deedie gudeman:
He's yirded, an' sae are the sorrows o' Nan.

An' that is a mither, wha gaed to the bad—
The curse o' her hame, baith to lassie and lad;
For she drank an' she pawned, but, thanks be to Gude!
Was drawn juist in time oot the black burnin' flood.

Aneath the white mutches there's mony a broo,
Wan, wallow't, an' runklet, an dowie yenoo;
Was ance like the lily, an' gowden an' sheen,
The lovelocks that shaded the bonnie blue een.

There's mony a heid that was black as the craw,
Or broun as the berry, noo white as the snaw,
The speerit inside, that's the gist o' the matter—
The heid's the ootside o' the cup an' the platter.

God bless ye, aul' grannies! I wish ye a' weel,
Ye're wearin' awa' to the lan' o' the leal;
May ye in the lan' o' the leal an' the true
Meet the aul' blin' grannie that sings to ye noo !

Kind shepherds wha watch wi' benevolent care
Owre the puir o' the flock—wha stint na nor spare
In labours o' love—ye are blest in your deed;
We honour, an' thank ye, an' bid ye God speed.

We bless ye, kind gentles, an' leddies sae fair,
That oot o' yer plenty hae something to spare
For white-heided grannies. O may it be given
To gentles an' grannies to meet yet in Heaven!

EPITHALAMIUM.

COMPOSED AND WRITTEN ON THE MARRIAGE OF JAMES ADDIE, ESQ.,
VIEWPARK, BOTHWELL, WITH JULIA WAKEFIELD, EASTWOODPARK,
RENFREW; AND INSCRIBED TO THE NEWLY-MARRIED PAIR.

HARK! the festal cannons boom:
Banish brooding, care, and gloom;
Happy looks and smiles assume
    On this auspicious day:
Ringing cheers give welcome high,
Pealing guns give loud reply,
Streaming flags salute the sky,
    And on the breezes play.

Cease hot labour for a while;
Frolic round each flaming pile;
On each bronzed cheek a smile
    Of pleased emotion glows;
Circling round the tow'ring flames,
Loud each jubilant cheer proclaims
Love and honour to the names
    The nuptial bands enclose!

Hail and welcome, happy pair!
Manly form, and lady fair:
Bright the home dear hands prepare;
   Come, gentle lady, come.
To the verdant banks of Clyde,
Hand in hand, and side by side,
The bridegroom leads his gentle bride—
   The angel of his home.

Home! sweet home, the gentle sway
Of sweet woman leads the way
To love and peace. Be yours, for aye,
   A happy blissful home.
Welcome as the flowers in May,
Lady, such is thine to-day;
Welcome, pure and bright as they,
   With May's sweet blossoms come.

Loving welcomes, true and kind,
Lady, it is thine to find,
In the new-found ties that bind
   In bonds of kindred love.
Lady, take the gift I bring—
Violet wreaths, the birth of spring,
Simple as the strain I sing,
   In hope thou wilt approve.

THE GOD OF THE SEASONS.

O GOD of the Seasons! we bring
To Thee our thankoff'rings of praise ;
We soar with the lark ; as we sing,
The skies shall re-echo our lays,
To us fruitful seasons Thou giv'st,
Thou gives the bright sunshine and rain,
And food to each creature that lives,
To satisfy, nourish, sustain.

Spring comes like a beautiful child—
Shy, timid, afraid to come forth ;
Oft smiling, oft sullen, and wild,
In gales from the east and the north.
The full swelling buds she expands,
She opens the infantine blooms ;
She calls—at the touch of her hand
They rise from their dark wintry tombs !

The Summer, in mantle of flowers,
Rose-crown'd, with the grace of a queen ;
Sweet choristers sing in her bowers,
With music of streamlets between.
The Sun, in his chariot of fire,
Speeds o'er the blue pathway above ;
His fervours all nature inspire
With harmony, beauty, and love.

Grave Autumn, with motherly care,
Spreads out with a bountiful hand
For her children enough and to spare
From the full-ripen'd fruits of the land.
The sere leaves are dropping—the flowers
Are faded.   How soothing the balm
She sheds o'er the fields and the bowers !
How sweet, yet how solemn the calm !

Stern Winter ! wild warfare to wage,
His legions leads out of the north ;
His storm-trumpet sounds to engage,
As howling and fierce they go forth.
Fair Nature, cold frozen and dead,
At the feet of her foe is lying ;
A snowdrift to cover her head,
And her darlings around her dying !

R

O God of the Seasons ! to Thee
Ascribe we all blessing and love ;
Each change of the seasons we see
Thy wisdom and goodness still prove.
Unchanging in purpose and power,
Unchanging in truth and in grace ;
O grant us when change is no more,
To dwell in the light of Thy face.

LINES

ADDRESSED TO MR. JAMES MUIR, SUMMERLEE IRONWORKS, ON THE
DEATH OF HIS TWO DAUGHTERS, WHO DIED WITHIN A FEW MONTHS
OF EACH OTHER.

FAIR garden of my life, my children's home,
With what full-hearted joy I used to come,
And there within the dear enclosure meet
My beauteous blossoms—there with fondness greet
My tender olive plants when ranged around
The board, with love and peace and blessing crowned.
O ye fair blossoms of my life and love,
I deemed not the dark cloud that lowered above
The garden of my life would burst in storm
First on thy fair young head and graceful form,
My new-blown rose, just opening to the day,
While yet the dew on thy green branches lay,
Struck by the fever simoom's scorching breath—
Laid withered, prostrate, in the dust of death.
Yet I, while weeping o'er thy buried dust,
Have, in the faith of an immortal trust,
A hope to meet thee in that blissful home,
Where sorrow, death, and tears shall never come.

Alas! not long my vision of delight
Had vanished, when again the deadly blight
Fell on my garden.   I had nourished there
A budding lily—fragrant, sweet, and fair—
Its snowy petals sparkling with the dew
Of life's young morn.   Near to my heart it grew;
But, ah! the spoiler came and tore
From my fond heart, that bleeds for evermore,
My tender lily; drooping in the storm
That bowed to death her fair and fragile form.

   I mourn my vanished flowers, my garden's pride;
Pleasant in life, death did not long divide
The sister blossoms, blighted in their bloom,
Now in the dark recesses of the tomb
Laid side by side, in calm and dreamless sleep.
My God, thy will be done!   Yet, while I weep,
I fain would wipe the tears that often flow
Down thy pale cheeks, dear partner of my woe—
The tender mother—she who reared with care
Her budding flow'rets into blossoms fair.
They faded on her bosom—passed the bourne
From whence to us they never will return;
But we to them in God's good time will come—
Where blossoms never die—"to Heaven our Home."

GRANNIE MIRK.

A STIRLING GRANNIE.

A CLEVER young dominie—noo in a kirk—
Was keepin' a schule near to auld Grannie Mirk—
A couthie auld grannie as e'er ye micht fin',
She wadna be idle, though feckly gane blin'.

Her heid was weel stockit wi' gude common sense—
In ilk' thing she did there was kindness an' mense:
To clashes an' clavers she wadna gae heed,
But ne'er was she hainin' to bodies in need.

Whan bairnies to schule wad come dreepin' wi' rain,
She dried the wat duds o' ilk puir droukit wean;
At her weel-beetit fire and cozie fire-en'
She gather'd the bairns like an auld clockin'-hen.

An' aft at twal'-oors, to auld grannie's fireside,
The dominie cam' for a weeock to bide;
A crumpie ait farle, wi' butter weel spread,
She gied him, an' wow but the chappie was glad.

Oor grannie was juist a real auld-warl' wife,
An' butter'd her cakes wi' an auld-fashion'd knife,
An' that was nae ither but grannie's ain thoom;
But the chiel bein' yaup, ne'er thocht o' the coom.

Noo the schule it is skail'd, an' grannie's gane hame,
An' the dominie's ekit D.D. to his name;
An' lang may he bruck a' the honours he's won,
The goal be as bricht as the race he has run.

A HAMILTON GRANNIE.

As she lay on her bed, frail dowie, an' dune,
The neebors a' thocht that her en' wad be sune;
That mornin' a gent had cum in frae the toun
To speir for her weelfare, an' sat himsel' doun.

" Hoo's a' wi' ye, grannie? an' whan did ye hear
Frae Davie, yer son? it's o' him I wad speir,
Wha has travell'd sae far through forest an' flood,
Wi' his life in his haun, for the hale warl's gude.

" Thou art blest amang mithers; nae leddy or queen
Has gi'en sic a son to the kintra, I ween;
He's an honour to Scotlan', an' lang afterhen'
He's laid in the mools, he'll be blest amang men."

Auld grannie lay still, sae contentit to hear
The praise o' her son sae duteous an' dear;
She leuk'd in his face, and said—" Bide ye a wee,
I've something o' Davie's will please ye to see."

" Gae Jeanie, my dochter," then grannie began,
" Bring Davie's hauf-croon, its the first that he wan;
A studgel bit callan he brocht it to me—
' That's the erles o' mair, my mither,' quo' he.

An' mony lang years after he gied me this,
My Davie cam' back, his auld mither to bless,
Frae far-awa' lan's, whaur the black bodies bide,
An' fock gied him welcome wi' pleasure an' pride.

" They honour'd an' prais'd him, an' gowpens o' gowd
They gather'd for him, an' right freely bestow'd ;
Then swith to his ain mither's dwallin' he's gaun
Wi' the twa-thousan' cheque they laid in his haun.

" He stood at my knee, an' he there laid it doon—
' O, dinna ye min' o' yer Davie's hauf croon !
The first that he wrocht for ? noo, see what is there ;
I tauld ye that it was the erles o' mair.'

" Noo, tak' the bit siller intil yer ain haun,
It's precious to me, ye may weel unnerstaun ;
It's no a' the siller in kintra an' toun
Wad tempt me to pairt wi' my Davie's hauf-croon."

Noo grannie sleeps soun' in the caul' bed o' death ;
On dear Davie's bosom she drew her last breath.
Again he's on travel ; may God be his guide ;
Bless a' his sair labours, protect an' provide !

LINES

COMPOSED AT THE REQUEST OF A VERY DEAR FRIEND, WHO WAS
SUFFERING FROM HEAVY GRIEF AND ANXIETY OF MIND.*

O EARTH! abode of grief and sin,
Whose miseries with life begin,
And follow us till lodged within
    The grave.

Oppress'd with woe, consumed by care,
Thy pleasures I did never share;
Now all my earthly wishes are
    A grave.

Oft have I view'd with longing eyes
Yon hallow'd spot where tombstones rise,
And bless'd the place which thus supplies
    A grave.

Pleasant to me is death's dark gloom;
Ye peaceful tenants of the tomb,
I long with you to make my home
    The grave.

* This piece was composed when the Authoress was about seventeen
years of age.

I know corruption and the worm,
The cold decaying ghastly form,
Are thine—but then, no strife, no storm,
                    Calm grave!

Oh ! I am weary—I would rest
Within thy cold and silent breast,
Nor rise till called to join the blest,
                    O grave!

Farewell, vain world, not worth a tear ;
Jesus alone my soul holds dear ;
Possessed of Him I cannot fear
                    The grave.

AULD MITHER SCOTLAN'.

A LAY OF THE DORIC.

Na, na, I wunna pairt wi' that,
   I downa gi'e it up;
O' Scotlan's hamely mither tongue
   I canna quat the grup.
It's 'bedded in my very heart,
   Ye needna rive an' rug;
It's in my e'e an' on my tongue,
   An' singin' in my lug.

O leeze me on the Scottish lass,
   Fresh frae her muirlan' hame,
Wi' gowden or wi' coal-black hair,
   Row'd up wi' bucklin'-kame;
Or wavin' roun' her snawy broo,
   Sae bonnie, braid, an' brent,
Gaun barefit wi' her kiltit coat,
   Blythe singin' ower the bent.

I heard her sing " Auld Robin Gray,"
    An' " Yarrow's dowie den"—
O' Flodden, an' oor forest flouris
    Cut doon by Englishmen ;
My saul was fir'd, my heart was fu',
    The tear was in my e'e :
Let ither lan's hae ither sangs,
    Auld Scotlan's sangs for me.

What words mair tender, kin', an' true,
    Can wooer ha'e to say,
Whan doun the burn at gloamin' fa',
    He meets his bonnie May?
Or words mair sweet, mair saft an' dear,
    Can lassie ha'e to speak,
Whan love is dancin' in her e'e
    An' glowin' on her cheek ?

For, oh, the meltin' Doric lay,
    In cot or clachan sung,
The words that drap like hinny dew
    Frae mither Scotlan's tongue,
Ha'e power to thrill the youthfu' heart
    An' fire the patriot's min' ;
To saften grief in ilka form,
    It comes to human kin'.

I saw a waefu' mither kneel
  On weary, tremblin' knee,
Beside the cradle, where she laid
  Her bairnie doon to dee.
An' aye she kissed the cauld white cheek,
  An' aye she made her mane,
" My ain wee lamb, my ain sweet doo,
  Frae me for ever gane !"

The faither straikit back her hair,
  An dichtit saft her een,
" Wee Willie's gane, thy marrow's here,
  Thy life-lang, lovin' frien'."
She leant her on his faithfu' breast,
  An' sabb'd " Wilt thou forgi'e
My sinfu' grief for bairnie lost,
  Whan I ha'e God an' thee ?"

" My mither, tho' the snaws o' eld
  Are on my pow an' thine.
My heart is leal to thee as in
  The days o' auld langsyne.
Thy hamely worth, thy couthie speech,
  Are dear—hoo dear to me !
An' neist to God, my John, an' bairns,
  Thy place sall ever be."

BE PITIFUL.

Be pitiful, be pitiful,
  Pity the weak and worn ;
Pity the outcast vile,
  Ever so lost and lorn.
Pity the poor who groan beneath
  Poverty's heavy load—
Treading with bleeding feet
  Life's dark and thorny road.

We pity the heathen abroad—
  Woe for heathen at home ;
Cry of perishing souls
  Into our ears has come.
Brothers' blood to frowning heaven
  Is crying from the ground—
Ignorance, vice, and crime
  Still increase and abound.

Be pitiful, be pitiful
 To children born in crime ;
Spawn of the slums, poor waifs,
 Cast on the stream of time.
These little bodies, shrivell'd, vile,
 Downtrodden in the mire,
Hold each a priceless gem,
 A spark of living fire.

Like Him who came to seek and save
 The lost, we would rescue ;
Seek the lost gem, and light
 The dying spark anew ;
From the deep pit and miry clay
 Where they embedded lie—
Reach down, and lift them up
 Ere they shall sink and die.

Pitiful, oh, how pitiful,
 To see our thousands sink ;
Oh lost, how lost, o'erwhelmed
 In foaming floods of drink !
The life-boat launch, and ply the oars
 With strong and tireless hand ;
Rescue, if not the whole,
 Bring all you may to land.

We gaze through tears on ghastly forms
   Cast by the stormy waves
On life's dark shores, immured
   In timeless, nameless graves.
Oh, pitying Heaven, look down,
   And bid the waves be still !
We toil too oft in vain,
   Though working with a will.

I asked a learned sheriff, whence
   Our crimes and evils flow—
Their causes and effects
   You in your place must know.
" I've found," he said, " the direful cause
   Of such effects, and think,
Exceptions being few,
   The cause is ever Drink."

THE ANGEL'S TREASURE.*

THERE stude a wee house on a lanely muirside,
Whaur mony lang years a puir widow did bide—
A decent, douce bodie, ne'er kenn'd to complain,
Or mak' a puir mouth to a neebor or frien'.

Her four bits o' bairns could dae naething ava,
An' sae their puir leevin' was scanty an' sma';
Their cleedin' was bare, an' nae shoon on their feet,
An' whiles the puir things hadna muckle to eat.

In simmer an' hairst she wad toil in the fiel';
Content if her bairnies had bread an' a biel';
In winter aye spinnin', sae eident an' thrang,
An' to cheer them at times wad lilt a bit sang.

Ae winter, puir bodie! in straits she had been,
An' was plying her wheel on a Saturday e'en;
Her hasp maun be spun, an' sauld to get meat,
Or on Monday the bairns wad hae naething to eat.

Sair bent on the spinnin', she heard nae the chime
O' the wag-at-the-wa' whan ringin' the time,
At twa in the mornin'—O horror an' wae!
To think she had broken the blest Sabbath-day!

* The writer's aged mother had this story from an old woman who
knew the widow referred to.

Alane she sat mournin' her sinfu' mishap,
There cam' on the winnock a gentle tap-tap,
An' a gentle voice said, " Puir carcase o' clay !
O, why hast thou broken the Lord's blessed day ?

" But dinna be frichten'd ; come oot, follow me,
I'll lead you to something that's gi'en unto thee ; "
An' she thocht that saft voice can come frae nae ill—
It speaks for the Sabbath, sae follow I will.

She open'd the door, an' saw doun by the dyke
A something, but kenn'd nae weel what it was like ;
She follow'd the shape, an' had nae fear ava,
Till close at the side o' an aul' ruin'd wa'—

Wi' ivy an' brambles, maist hidden frae sicht,
Were the crum'lin' stanes, but she saw by the licht
O' the mune that a stane was drawn oot o' the wa'—
Her heart gied a loup at the neist thing she saw.

There fell oot a pig fu' o' siller an' gowd ;
" Tak' it up," said the shape, " on thee it's bestow'd ;
That treasure was hidden, lang ages agane,
In that moulderin' wa', an noo its thine ain.

" Thy trust was in God an' thine ain willin' arm ;
Still trust in His 'gudeness, He'll shield thee frae harm
The stay o' the widow an' orphan is He :
Fareweel, I nae longer may tarry wi' thee."

S

She liftit her een, but the shape it was gane ;
She hearken'd, but hearin' or voice there was nane ;
She leuk'd to the sky, wi' a tear in her e'e,
" Gude Lord! has Thy angel been watchin' owre me ?

" For this Thou has gi'en me, Thy name I will praise ;
My bairns will get schulin', be fed, an' get claes ;
An', as lang as I leeve, fu' brawly we'll fen'.
Wha trusts Thee in need, sall be blest in the en'."

ADDRESS TO GARIBALDI
IN HIS RETIREMENT AT CAPRERA, 1868.

Lone dweller of the stony isle!
Dost thou at fortune's caprice smile,
Soars thy great mind above thy state,
Serene amid the shocks of fate?
Thou art a king! thou reign'st in all
The hearts that bound at freedom's call!
Though now the shades of Papal night
With deeper gloom obscure the light
Of freedom human and divine,
The day will dawn, the light will shine,
The shadows fly, the gazing world
Shall see her standard broad unfurled
On Rome's proud walls, men freed from thrall,
In haste, at her stern trumpet call,
Assume the rights so long withheld,
By legions leagued their chains to weld;
Then freedom, link'd to sacred truth,
Shall give to man, and teach to youth,
Heaven's simple "unencumber'd plan"
To rule, govern, and save the man.
   Oh! why, like hermit in his cell,
Dost thou in lone Caprera dwell,

While there is work to do abroad—
The work of man, the work of God?
To work aright there must be given
The time, the place, the power from heaven.
Man, working with his fellow-man,
To execute a self-formed plan,
Mistakes his way, his time and power,
And rushes in an evil hour
On scenes of slaughter and defeat,
And finds his plans were incomplete.
Freedom of State is part, not whole;
For we would free the enslavèd soul,
Would break the fetters that enchain
The soul to superstitions vain.
O'er these the sword no power can have—
It opens not the living grave
Where prison'd souls in bondage lie:
This is the work of God most high.
He in His wisdom forms the plan;
His chosen instrument is man,
To bear the torch of Truth abroad
Wherever darkness hath abode;
To scare the demons into flight,
And shed around supernal light.

    Thou warrior brave! thou chief beloved!
Thy valour has been well approved
On many a bloody battle field,
Where foes were forced to fly or yield.

Yet I would twine around thy brow
A fresher, fairer wreath than thou
Hast ever won, or worn in war,
With freedom's foes, to drive afar
The Bourbon tyrant from the land
That groan'd beneath his ruthless hand.
Would'st thou thy loved Italia see
United, prosperous, and free?
Then know this ne'er can be attained
Though sword, and arm, and nerve be strained
In hottest warfare in the cause
Of civil freedom. I must pause.
Ere I conclude, the good is gained,
While yet the Papacy retained
A power to hold, control, and bind
In slavish bonds the warriors' mind.
Let them, let all, with candour true,
The Scriptures search—to God is due
The soul's allegiance. Homage pay
To Him alone. The glorious day
Of truth revealed, with hallowed light
Shall chase the shades of Papal night;
Then shall thy loved Italia be
United, prosperous, and free.

AUTUMN WINDS.

THE Autumn gales are blowing,
   And wrecks bestrew the shore;
The angry ocean rages
   With loud and wild uproar.
Furious billows leeward
   The doomèd vessels bore;
Their prey the foaming breakers
   To fragments madly tore.

The Autumn winds are singing
   The death-song of the leaves;
Shrill piping, as they winnow
   The shocks of golden sheaves.
Soft singing to the reaper,
   Who loves to hear the song,
And bares his dewy forehead,
   A they singing skim along.

The Autumn breeze is hushing
   To sleep the fading flowers ;
Breathing on the falling leaves
   And through the rifled bowers ;
Murmuring through the woodlands,
   And sighing in the pines ;
Light rippling on the streamlet
   In broken, wavy lines.

On a couch of fallen leaves—
   The golden and the brown—
While the breezes fan my brow,
   There I would lay me down.
Alone with God and nature,
   'Midst emblems of decay;
'Neath the calm Autumnal sky
   I'd breathe my life away.

SUMMER IS WANING.

SUMMER is waning, the roses are dead ;
Lilies, sweet violets, and hyacinths fled ;
Her fragrant blossoms the hawthorn has shed ;
Faded the cowslip ; and low on her bed
    The daisy is drooping and pale.
The sorrel's soft blossoms of pearly gloss
Hide in her cushion of green velvet moss ;
Bloomless the eglantine droops from the trees,
Her honeyèd breathings perfume not the breeze
    That murmurs and sighs through the vale.

Warblers are silent : the song of the thrush
Is hailing no more, from tree and from bush,
The soft summer dawn with roseate blush
Kindling the east with a crimsoning flush,
    Brightened with streamers of gold.
Grasshoppers chirrup no more in the grass ;
We hear not the humming of bees as they pass,
Nectar to drain from the sweet heather bells,
Storing their treasures in soft waxen cells,
    For winter, dark, cheerless, and cold.

Man ! when the rose of thy summer is dead,
When youth, with its flowers and pleasures are fled,
Blossoms that charm'd with their fragrance, all shed;
Time and decay shedding snow on thy head ;
    And thy brow grows wrinkled and pale.
Then when the roses and flowers of thy youth
Shall die, may blossoms of virtue and truth,
Deathless in beauty, and rich in perfume,
Cheer thee in life, and shed over thy tomb
    Sweet memories never to fail !

THE FEVER-CLOUD.

REMINISCENCES OF AN OUTBURST OF MALIGNANT FEVER IN ONE OF OUR
GARRISON TOWNS IN THE BEGINNING OF THE PRESENT CENTURY.

The fever-cloud hung owre the toun,
    Dark drippin' wi' the dews o' death,
That fell on mony a lowly hame
    Wi' silent, stealin,' deidly skaith.

There burnin,' ravin', moanin' lay
    The stricken faither an' the wife,
An' maybe bairnies twa or three
    Juist hingin' owre the verge o' life.

Sair fley'd, the neebors aft stude back :
    To tend the sick they daurdna gang,
For fear o' bein' ta'en themsel's,
    An' sae their ain at hame wad wrang.

But some wha ventured were preserv'd,
    An' afterhen were glad to think
Hoo they had rais'd the deein' heid,
    An' held to fever'd lips the drink.

The mourners ne'er were aff the streets ;
    An' ilka day the auld kirkyaird
Had open graves, an' mony mair
    New happit wi' the turn'd-up swaird.

An' aye the deidly fever-cloud
 Was hingin' owre the smitten toun ;
An' in the sodgers' barracks laid
 Hoo mony bauld, braw fallows doun!

Hoo aft the music o' the band,
 Sad, solemn, mournfu', thrill'd the air,
Whan marchin' wi' the funeral train
 That to the grave a comrade bare !

An' whan the fever cloud had pass'd,
 White were the cheeks an' howe the een
That leukit oot frae mony doors,
 Sair langin' for the fields sae green.

A dark dull house—a puir man's hame,
 Stude in the warst pairt o' the toun,
An' there his gude an' lovin' wife
 Lay wi' the fever stricken doun.

The fever-fire had burn'd her sair,
 Yet she cam' thro' an' gat the turn ;
But, oh ! her strength was gane, an' sae
 This pious dochter sair did mourn.

For in the neist bed there was laid
 Her aged faither, near to death,
An', whaur she lay, she heard a change
 Come wi' his gaspin', rattlin' breath.

Oh, noo, her heart was like to break,
 For she cou'd naither gang nor staun';
But, slippin' owre the bed, she tried
 To creep to him on knee and haun'.

The bed was laigh, an', as she knelt,
 She saw upon her faither's face—
Damp wi' the dews o' death—a gleam
 O' heavenly licht—the licht o' grace.

A whisper frae her quiv'rin' lips
 Fell on her deein' faither's ear—
" My faither, rests thy saul in peace ;
 For death is near—oh, very near ?"

He whisper'd low—" I rest in Christ—
 Nae shade o' doot for fifty years
Hath dimm'd my faith—He gives me peace ;
 Death hath nae sting, my saul nae fears."

" Bless me, my faither ;" an' she rais'd
 His haun' an' laid it on her head.
" My faither's God an' mine be yours,"
 In mutter'd, broken words he said.

A quiv'rin' spasm slightly stirr'd
 His lip an' cheek—a lang, deep sigh ;
He pass'd in peace, he gaed to rest—
 The Rest eternal in the sky.

Some twa-three hours had gane, an' syne
   Hame cam' the gudeman frae his wark;
His helpless wife lay near the bed,
   Whaur lay the faither stiff an' stark.

"Oh! Mary, what is this?" he said,
   An' liftit her intil the bed;
An' kin'ly neebors sune cam' in
   To tend the wife an' dress the dead.

Oh! Mary Lee, a faithfu' wife
   Thou wert—a dochter true an' kin';
In weal an' wae, in life an' death,
   Thy faither's God was ever thine.

AN APPEAL FOR THOMAS ELLIOT,

THE SHOEMAKER POET.

"POOR Tom's a-cold!"   Upon his shrinking head
The pelting storm beats pitiless!   On bed
Of languishing, disease, and cureless pain
He lies, surrounded by the haggard train
Of want—the victim of the thousand ills
With which cold poverty the life-blood chills.
Alas, poor Tom! must thy last look on earth
Fall on a squalid room and cheerless hearth,
Pale pining children, and a weeping wife,
With scanty sustenance for needs of life?
"Take physic, Pomp!"—good med'cine will be found
In that small room, with misery brooding round.
Time was when Tom invoked the Doric muse,
And she to hear his suit would not refuse,
And as he "bit the birse," and plied the awl,
The voice of song rung through the cobbler's stall:
And, while with sounding strokes he beat the leather,
His heart was with the muse "amang the heather."

   I mourn for thee, my brother!   Could thy weal
By me be compassed, I were quick to heal

Thy maladies, thy drooping spirits cheer,
In aiding those by thee beloved and dear !
Of gold and silver I, possessing none,
Give what I have ; and here I ask alone
Of you who have—Is it not on record
Who giveth to the poor lends to the Lord ?
A safe investment this !   You freely may
Lend to the Lord—He surely will repay.

ADDRESS

COL. D. C. R. CARRICK-BUCHANAN,

Of Drumpellier,

ON HIS PRESENTING, AS A FREE GIFT TO THE WORKING MEN OF COAT-
BRIDGE, A PARK, ORNAMENTED AND ENCLOSED, TO BE USED BY THEM
AS A PLACE OF RECREATION AND PLEASURE.—SEPT. 17, 1866.

HAIL! noble mind, that formed the liberal plan :
Hail! generous heart, that on the working man,
With kindly courtesy, this day bestowed
A valued boon ; while thousand bosoms glow'd
With grateful feeling.   May thy high intent
And noble purpose to its full extent
Be blest and gratified.   Thy willing aid,
Both past and present, be it ever paid
With honour, by the class whom thy design
Is to improve—to elevate—refine.
May high success attend thy every plan
To raise the *status* of the working man.

   And she, the gentle partner of thy life,
A gracious lady and a tender wife,

Whose loving charities so oft assuage
The pains of want, disease, and helpless age :
Who bids her teacher sway with gentle rule
The youthful pupils in the " Lady's School,"
All sacred truth upon their hearts to bind,
And " pour the fresh instruction o'er the mind."

     For this—for all—may ye, oh, honoured pair,
     Heaven's richest, choicest blessings ever share !

ADDRESS TO MRS. WM. ANDERSON *

ON THE EARLY DEATH OF HER ONLY SON.

" WE weep with those who weep :" I sympathise
With thee, oh mother ! with the mournful eyes
That speak, with sad, mute eloquence, a grief
That hath no tears—how oft the blest relief
Of woes less poignant.   Ah ! that grief of thine,
Craves for a higher sympathy than mine.
" Ask, and thou shalt receive ; seek, thou shalt find "
Balm for thy wounded heart, peace for thy mind,
In Him, the Man of Sorrows, who hath borne
Our griefs and sorrows ; comforts those who mourn.
HE giveth peace ; His peace He giveth *thee.*
And though thy cherished plant, a fair young tree,
Rich with the buds of promise, was laid low
Ere yet he blossomed in the sunny glow
Of life's bright summer,—'twas no cruel hand
That cut, with sudden stroke, the filial band,
Unloosed "the silver cord," and bore on high
Thy tender plant to gardens of the sky.
And thou, when laid aside this " mortal coil,"
Art, too, transplanted to celestial soil,
With the dear partner of thy heart and life,
Who shared thy sorrow, watched with thee the strife

* Wife of Rev. Dr. Wm. Anderson, Glasgow.

Of sinking nature with her mortal foe,
Till she succumbed beneath thy deadly blow,
Relentless death! and with one long, low sigh,
The conflict ended—Mother! thou wert nigh:
The silent anguish, deep, yet tearless woe
That pierced thy swelling heart, thy God did know,
When the bright angel, watching o'er thy boy,
Bore from the couch of death to realms of joy
The young immortal.—He, the loved, revered—
The Father, too, was nigh; in faith prepared,
His Isaac, child of promise, to resign,
Saying, "Thy will be done, oh God, not mine!"
Blest parents, ye who bow beneath the rod,
Resign'd, submissive to the will of God;
For yet a little while, and ye shall see,
Beneath the shade of Life's immortal Tree,
The cherished plant ye reared on earth with care—
Rich in full blossom'd glory, green and fair;
Then ye, blest *trio*, death's dark valley trod,
Shall blossom in the paradise of God.

TO WILLIAM LOGAN,

On the Death of his aged Mother.

Mourn not, my Christian friend :—thy late removed,
Thy sainted mother, cherished and beloved,
In Jesus fell asleep.—Oh sorrow not
As those who have no hope ! Be ne'er forgot
The hand Divine, that to thy filial love
Consigned the sacred trust.—God will approve
The watchful care, the tender, pious zeal,
The ceaseless ministrations to her weal
With which thou sought'st her helpless age to guard,
And pour into thy bosom rich reward—
Yet oft thine eye will glance, thine ear will strain,
As if to see the form revered again ;
As if once more the feeble voice to hear ;
A mother's voice for ever true and dear.
The couch is empty, and the voice is gone ;
Thou standest by her vacant chair alone :
Yet not alone, thy mother's God and thine
Sets in this cloud of tears the bow divine—
The rainbow of His promise, fair and free ;
According to thy day thy strength shall be.

And she, the partner of thy life and heart,
She who in all thy sorrows bears a part—
And he, thy tender plant, thy duteous boy,
May both with thee through lengthened years enjoy
The tranquil bliss of calm domestic love,
And blest re-union in the home above!

TO WILLIAM CRAIG,

ON THE DEATH OF AN ONLY SON, WHO LOST HIS LIFE BY A
RAILWAY ACCIDENT.

'TWAS drear November; by the turbid tide
That foaming chafes the wintry banks of Clyde,
I saw a careworn man with mournful air;
And thus he spoke his woe while straying there—
" My son, my son, I thought not thus to part;
Stay of my life and treasure of my heart.
A goodly tree he grew up by my side ;
And I beheld, with all a parent's pride,
The verdant boughs, beneath whose grateful shade
I hoped to find repose when strength would fade.
And she, the tender mother too, would share
His filial love and ever duteous care.
But ah! the anguish we were doomed to feel
When he from 'neath the steam car's gory wheel
Was drawn with crushed and mangled limbs to lie,
Far from his home, to suffer and to die.
He died, but not alone—there daily moved
Around his couch the parents so beloved ;
Calm and resigned he yielded up his breath,
And passed in faith and hope the gates of death.

And ye, oh mourning pair, by grief oppressed ;
Bereaved of him your youngest, dearest, best,
Look up to God! He comforts all who mourn ;
Your son has passed the bourne whence none return.
But saved by grace, and called by God to come,
To meet, and dwell with him in " Heaven our home."

THE ENEMY IN THE GATE.

To Britannia.

Nay, all this availeth thee nothing—
   Thy prestige, thy power, and estate,
Thy glory, honour, and riches;
   An enemy sits in the gate.
Thy place 'mong the nations is highest;
   Britannia, thou sitt'st as a Queen:
Unequalled in commerce—in warfare
   Unrivall'd thy conquests have been.

The seed of the Word ever sowing,
   Thou toilest still early and late;
Yet all this availeth thee nothing,
   Thy enemy sits in the gate.
Thy charities great and abundant
   Relief to the needy dispense;
To open the portals of knowledge,
   Unsparing of time and expense.

Yet all this availeth thee nothing—
   Thy commerce, thy conquests, and state,
Thy charities, teachings, and sowings,
   Thy enemy sits in the gate.
For in thee for ever abideth
   A demon, most potent and fell,
The land is bestrewn with his victims,
   His slain, who their numbers may tell?

The cup of deep anguish he brimmeth,
   For parents bemoaning the fate
Of sons in the clutch of the demon,
   Who sits evermore in the gate.
The wife often steepeth her pillow
   With tears, as she listens by night
The voice and the tread of the demon,
   Whose breath sheddeth cursing and blight.

He filleth the jail and the workhouse
   With numbers astounding and great;
He feedeth the hulks and the gibbet,
   And still he sits fast in the gate.
On children, pale, ragged, and famish'd,
   He blows with his pestilent breath,
They wither, and wander in darkness,
   And pine in the shadows of death.

We struggle to vanquish the demon,
   To banish him furth of the State,
To save from perdition his victims,
   But still he sits fast in the gate.
So all this availeth us nothing,
   While revenue coffers he fills
With gold, from his fiery Alembics,
   Distillery coppers and stills.

Avaunt thee! dread Demon, avaunt thee!
   Too long we have courted our fate,
Drunk deep of thy cup of enchantment,
   And, perishing, fell in the gate.
Britannia, who lately deliver'd
   The captives of dark Theodore,
Has captives by thousands in bondage,
   The captives of Drink, on her shore.

SKETCHES OF VILLAGE CHARACTER
IN DAYS "O' LANGSYNE."

I've aften been thinkin', whan sittin' alane,
Blin', dowie, an' cowerin' upon the hearth stane,
On places an' faces I ken'd o' langsyne ;
Lang, lang oot o' e'e sicht, but ne'er oot o' min'.

Sae clear they are written on memory's page,
That nouther the failin's nor frailties o' age
Can score oot the writin', or dicht it awa' ;
My heart is aye young, tho' my heid's like the snaw.

It's towmonds three-score since my couthie auld man
An' mysel' were made ane, an' we settl't a plan
That aye we hae follow't, an' ne'er sall forget,
To be warkrife, an' honest, an' haud oot o' debt.

An' aft I teuk notes, as I jogit alang
The rough road o' life that a' wark bodies gang,
O' what was gaun on, what was said an' was dune ;
An' some o' thae jottin's ye'll hear aboot sune.

Frae the village I've leev'd in maist feck o' my life,
A glaikit wee lassie, a maid, an' a wife ;
Some sketches, tho' hamely, yet truthfu' I'll draw
O' the times an' the bodies lang vanish't awa'.

I.

An' sae I'll begin wi' the rev'rend John Bouir ;
By ilk ane that ken'd him belov'd to this hour :
It's years forty-five since he gade to his rest ;
His mem'ry is blessed, he rests wi' the blest.

Oor ain parish minister—forty years lang—
In wark for his Maister aye eident an' thrang ;
A workman still richtly dividin' the truth,
As their needs wad require, to age an' to youth.

It wad dune yer heart gude, to see him come thro'
The thrang to the poopit, wi' grace on his broo—
A herald o' mercy, commission'd by God
To point us to heaven, an' guide on the road.

An' aye thro' the parish ilk year he wad gang
In due visitation, nor thocht the road lang,
Whan gaun to examine, exhort, an' reprove,
Or sit by the sick like an angel o' love.

Wi' bairns in his marriage he never was blest ;
A young orphan laddie he teuk to his breast,
An' foster'd, an' bred up, wi' faitherly care—
Grew up to his sorrow, a grief an' a snare.

His auntie, the mistress, aft stude him in stead,
An' ne'er said that black was the e'e in his heid ;
The minister sairly was troubled in mind,
An' weel it was ken'd hoo he griev'd an' repined.

The end it cam' sune, an' that endin' was ill :
The lad was in something contrair'd in his will :
He ran into his room, an' loudly he swore
That his life he wad tak—an' lockit the door.

The minister tremil't, and shook like a leaf,
An' ran to the door, fu' o' terror an' grief :
Oh ! horror ! he saw, creepin' oot neath the door,
The red bluid, an' faintin', he fell on the floor !

They liftit him up in a sorrowfu' plicht ;
An' the wretch he cried oot, " I've gien him a fricht ;
I think he'll ne'er try to contrair me again :"—
In his arm, wi' a knife, he had open'd a vein.

The gude man cam' roun', but whan gangin' aboot,
His stap it was feeble, his face like a clout ;
An' ne'er in the poopit again was he seen—
In less than a towmond his grave it was green.

We never hae had, we may ne'er hae again,
A minister like him—I say it wi' pain ;
Noo gude maister Bouir's wi' the weary at rest,
An' the wicked nae mair his peace will molest.

II.

There was Willie, the weaver, laigh in degree ;
An' puir as a man in his station maun be ;
Aye thin in the body, an' bruckle in health—
His hame it held naething that savoured o' wealth.

For there his ae dochter sat at the tambour;
An' there the auld pirn wheel gaed birrin' like stour;
An' there on his loom the gude weaver wad croon,
As it rattl't awa', some holy saum tune.

Yet in that laigh dwallin' the speerit o' grace,
An' sweet human kindness, was seen on ilk face;
An' sympathy true, o' the kindest an' best,
They had aye for the puir, the sick an' distress'd.

An elder in office lang time he had been,
An' weel he fulfill'd a' its duties, I ween;
An' mony that socht him, aneath his ain roof,
Gat counsel an' comfort, advice an' reproof.

Whaure'er there was sickness or death in a house,
They sent for gude Willie, the pious an' douce;
For aye he was ready, by nicht or by day,
To succour the sick, wi' the deein' to pray.

Whan neebors fell oot, an' wad bicker an' flyte;
An' women were fashous wi' clashes and spite;
To rede up their quarrels he mony times gaed,
In meekness an' wisdom peace aften he made.

An' Nannie, his wife—a true helpmeet was she,
Weel fitted gude counsel an' comfort to gi'e;
Weel skill'd in the ailments o' women an' weans,
To soothe them in sickness, an' saften their pains.

A mither in Israel sae truly was she
That het tears doun trickl'd frae mony an e'e
Amang us that sorrowfu' day she was ta'en ;
Sae skilfu', sae haunie, an' helpfu' was nane.

The elder he ne'er was the same man again ;
Fu' sairly he miss'd her, wha aye wad sustain
An' cheer him in duty whate'er micht betide ;
But sune cam' the time whan he lay by her side.

Ye've leuk'd on this picture, noo, leuk ye on that—
I've leuk'd on it aft till I sabbed an' grat—
It's years sixty-four since I open'd my een
On that picture, aye darker the langer it's seen.

Near five hunner bodies dwalt in oor wee toun,
An' five public-houses were 'mang us set doun ;
Frae them cam' to us the warst ills that befell ;
What cam' to the publican, here I maun tell.

III.

There was Lang Willie Gairner, an' Luckie, his wife,
An' Jean, the ae dochter, the pride o' their life ;
They're the first on my leet in the publican line ;
They lang hae been yirded, an' lang oot o' min'.

Whan first they began, they were fast makin' gear—
Had maist o' the custom an' maist o' the steer ;
Whan dances or sprees were gat up in the toun,
It was to Lang Willie's the youngsters gaed doun.

Whan big penny weddin's were held in the hoose,
O ! then Luckie Gairner grew cantie an' crouse ;
She dish'd up the kail, wi' the tatties an' beef ;
An' 'mang toddy brewers she aye was the chief.

Then the chiels wad begin to thump wi' their heels
On the floor—cryin' oot, " Mak' room for the reels ; "
An' they heez'd the blin' fiddler up to his stance—
" Play up," was the cry, as they boun' to the dance.

Sae fast an' sae dinsome the dancin' gaed on ;
The fiddle wad scream, an' the floor it wad groan,
Wi' jumpin' an' thumpin' o' merry gaun feet—
Then hey for the toddy, their whistles to weet !

The sun an' the lav'rock were baith in the lift
E're they thocht it was time their quarters to shift ;
Then Luckie was ca'd, an' the lawin' was settl't,
Tho' aften the siller was mair than they ettl't.

Noo, Luckie, some time, had been layin' her lugs
In whisky, an' drank it in tumblers an' jugs ;
An' sae ye may ken that her life was sune sped—
Ae morning they found her cauld deid in her bed.

Syne Willie grew donnert wi' sorrow an' drink ;
In poortith an' pain to the grave he did sink ;
An' Jean, the ae dochter, had gane a grey-gate,
An naebody cared to speer after her fate.

IV.

The neist that I ha'e on the publican's leet
Ne'er dream'd in a beuk wi' the public to meet ;
Tho' keepin' a public, his wits he had tint
At thocht o' himsel' an' his public in print.

A bardie wee bodie was Sandie M'Craw,
Wi' his stowsie gudewife, weel dinkit an' braw ;
Their public was stockit wi' a' kin's o' drink—
They turn'd a gude penny, as weel ye may think.

Their hoose was aye countit the best in the line ;
The tod-huntin' gentry aft cam' there to dine :
Wi' eatin' an' drinkin' they rais't sic a splore,
The hale hoose was ringin' wi' riot an' roar.

The weavin' was brisk, an' the prices were high ;
Whan wabs they were oot, an' the weavers were dry,
They slocken'd their drouth wi' a stoupie or twa—
An' the stoups were aft' fill'd by Sandie M'Craw.

The brothers Masonic, an' farmers sae gash,
An' a' that had pouches weel plenish't wi' cash,
Cam' swarmin' an' bummin' like bees to a byke ;
An' neebors were fash'd wi' the bizzin' an' fyke.

But thro' a' the habble, the steer, an' stramash,
Frien' Sandie was gath'rin' an' bankin' the cash ;
The sale o' the whisky was aye growin' mair—
An' that's the maist feck o' the publican's care !

U

Wi' fire in your bosom, you're sure to be burn'd ;
The fire it was beetit, the tide it was turn'd—
For Sandie had ta'en to the drinkin' himsel' ;
An' what was the ootcome o' that I maun tell :—

Ae mornin' the word ran like fire thro' the toun,
His gawsie gudewife in a fit had faun doun ;
Whan they liftit her up, an' on to the bed,
The breath it was gane, an' the speerit had fled.

Noo Sandie, wha aye thro' his hale wedded life
Had stude in some fear o' his managing wife,
Gaed a' to the bad ; an' he swill'd an' he drank,
Till sune in the grave o' the drunkard he sank.

V.

We come to the third on oor leet, Johnnie Gibb,
Wi' his wife, snuffie Jean, sae bardie an' glib ;
They keepit a public some years in oor toun,
Till their heels gaed up, an' the public gaed doun.

Whan Jock an' his wife were dementit wi' drink ?
They wad quarrel an' strike, an', what wad ye think,
Wi' shoolfu's o' fire, on the loan they wad chase
Ilk-ither—unheeding the shame an' disgrace.

They had four bits o' bairns ; the ill-tentit things
Were fu' o' the ills that sic parentage brings ;
They wad fill their wee juggies wi' whisky an swill,
An' stoiter aboot till they fell an' lay still.

Twa dochters were married—waesucks for the men!
Wi' drink they began, an' in drink they did en';
An' Jock, their ae brither, a vogie young chiel,
Wi' drink was owrecome an' left deid on the fiel'.

VI.

It's threescore o' towmonds, an' maybe it's mair,
Since first I set een on an' auld fashion'd pair,
Wha keepit a public lang years in oor toun;
They teuk to the drinkin' an' drank themsel's doun.

The man he was ill, but the wife she was waur,
On her wizen'd-like face was mony a scar,
For they focht like twa cocks, an' aft she was seen
Gaun stoiten aboot wi' a pair o' black een.

Whan the barrels were toom the sign was taen doun;
The wife gaed deleerit an' frichtet the toun,
An' never was heard sic a din an' deray
As rang through the publican's dwallin' that day.

The crystal an' crockery she dang a' to smash,
The jars an' the bottles gaed doun wi' a crash;
An' the stoups, big an' wee, she ran thro' the fire,
An' brak' a' the lozens afore she wad tire.

Whan she cou'd dae nae mair she fell an' lay still;
An' the man, hoo he swore her bluid he wad spill;
But the neebors cam' in frae murder to 'fend:
I've tauld hoo they leev'd, ye may guess at their end.

VII.

An' there was Tam Wilson, and Mysie his wife—
Wi' heids growin' grey, on the dounhill o' life ;
They're the fifth an' the last that staun' on my leet ;
An' wow but I'm tir'd till the count is complete.

The feck o' Tam's whisky cam' thro' the wee stell ;
But Mysie was aye sae auld farrant an' snell,
She cheatit the gauger, and laughed in his face ;
Her drink it was countit the best in the place.

The couple had ne'er ony bairns o' their ain ;
An' that was a blessing—wi' sorrow an' pain
I think o' the lessons the public-hoose bairn
Is aften sae able and willin' to learn.

They had a bit grun', an' they keepit a coo,
An' it wasna lang time till a' was gane thro' :
For Mysie aft liftit her haun' to her mouth,
An' nocht but the whisky wad slocken Tam's drouth.

They gaed fast doun the hill, their custom fell aff ;
Their hoose it was haunted by a' the riff-raff,
Wha watch'd weel the time whan Mysie was fou ;
An' mony a lawin' her haun' never drew.

Syne Tam teuk his deid-ill, an' whan he was gane,
Auld Mysie was left in the hoose a' her lane,
But sune she gaed after—ae grave hauds them baith :
My leet noo is endit, and sae I'll tak' breath.

Like Bunyan's first pilgrim, maist chokin' for breath,
Thro' the noisome valley an' shadow o' death,
I seem to hae gane, in the coorse o' my leet;
The flames aften scaith'd me an' blister'd my feet.

The bairn that is burn'd will ha'e dread o' the fire;
An' oh! gin I had my ain will and desire,
There's a fire I wad droon an' quench evermair—
A fire that has burn'd me richt aften an' sair.

That fire is the spirit that rins frae the stell;
An' what it consumes there's nae mortal can tell:
Like the fire that's neer quench'd, the worm that neer
        dies,
There's weepin' an' wailin' whare'er it may rise.

Let naebody think that I coudna sae mair,
Whan rivin' the rags aff oor muckle plague-sair,
That eats like a cancer, an' poisons oor blood,
Mak's rags o' oor cleedin', an' preys on oor food.

Oh, mony a lazy an' drucken young loon,
'Mang weavers, wha aye were the bulk o' oor toun,
Teuk the shillin', an' march'd wi' the sodgers awa'—
To fecht wi' auld Bony whaur mony did fa'.

The war it was endit, the weavin' grew scant,
The puir weaver bodies were aften in want,
Sae sma' were their win'in's, wi' bairns an' a wife,
It pinched them richt sairly to haud in their life.

Cou'd wives in the present see what I hae seen,
They wad get a lesson richt needfu', I ween;
Nocht ken they o' hainin' the meat an' the siller,
In strong tea an' toddy ne'er droonin' the miller.

A drap parritch an' milk, wi' tatties an' saut—
Wi' that the puir weaver ne'er faund muckle faut,
A coarse cutty coat, wi' a short-goon an' brat,
Was a' the wife's cleedin', an' thankfu' for that.

As the weavin' grew waur, the shops they wad toom,
An' the weavers in scores gaed aff frae the loom
To seek ither wark ; they were tired in the strife
O' strugglin' an' starvin' the hale o' their life.

An' noo ye may gang thro' the length o' oor toun,
The loom ye'll ne'er hear, in a name or a soun' ;
The men o' the furnace, the forge, an' the mine,
Tak' the place o' the weavers in days o' langsyne.

Amang a' the changes oor toun has gane thro',
There's nae change in ae thing, that's drinkin', I trow ;
We drink, but our drouth is ne'er slocken'd ; I think,
The higher the wages the deeper we drink.

Wi' woe an' wi' wailin' I send up a cry,
That enters the ears o' the Holy an' High :
Oh save my ain Scotlan', oh stem the dark flood,
That droons her an' a' that is holy an' gude !

THE GREETIN' BAIRN.

A LEGEND OF LUGGIE BURN (LANGLOAN.)

Wow, Maggie, hae ye seen a ghaist?
   Your maist as white as ane yoursel,'
Wi' een like wull-cats glowerin' wild,
   What awsome tale hae ye to tell?

I saw ye at the gloamin' fa',
   Gaun linkin' doun by Luggie burn,
Juist whaur aroun' the eerie howm,
   Ca'd Spunkie Howe, it taks a turn.

Speak, woman, tell what ye hae seen;
   Was it some black uncanny thing?
Or was it Spunkie, eldritch elf,
   That owre ye did his glamour fling?

I canna say that ocht I saw
   O' bogle, ghaist, or worrikow,
That haunt, folk say, the eerie howm
   Whaur Spunkie dances in the howe.

I gaed to gather in my claes
   That bleachin' lay by Luggie burn,
But ere I wan the eerie howm
   I grew sae fley'd I thocht to turn.

But leukin' down, I saw the yirth
    New howkit frae the aul' thorn dyke,
An' thocht this maun hae been the wark
    O' Robin's moudie-huntin' tyke.

A gullie knife, a' roustit red,
    Had been turn'd up; I lootit doun,
An' took it up—sweet mercy! May
    My lugs ne'er hear sic fearsome soun'.

It rase frae 'mang my verra feet,
    I cou'dna steer frae whaur I stude,
It set my verra hair on en,'
    An' grue't an' chitter't thro' my bluid.

It was a wild, unyirthly skirl,
    Like some wee bairn in mortal pain;
At ilka skirl it louder grew,
    As if it nee'r wad stop again.

The knife fell frae my powerless haun',
    The skirlin' ceas'd, I heard na mair;
An' syne I faund my feet, an' ran
    For hame, like ony huntit hare.

Noo, Maggie, I cou'd wad a groat
    That ye hae faund the vera knife
Wi' whilk a puir misguided lass
    Had ta'en her new-born bairnie's life.

An' I ha'e heard my Grannie tell
    That whan a lass she teuk a turn
Ae nicht at een, to meet her Jo,
    Doun by the Luggie's hauntit burn,

They dauner't up an' doun a while,
    But whan they turn'd the aul' dyke back
They heard the cryin' o' a bairn,
    That skirl'd as if it ne'er wad slack.

They leukit roun', but nocht cou'd see—
    Nae leevin' thing, nor bairn, nor beast,
But Grannie grippit fast her Jo,
    An' hid her face upon his breast.

They cou'dna lift their feet for fear,
    But sune as they gat power to rin,
They turn'd an' fled, as if for life,
    Dang up the door, an' swith gaed in.

The hoose was dark, the folk asleep,
    They stood a wee to tak' their breath ;
But Grannie swarf't, an' on the floor
    She fell as white an' caul' as death.

He rais'd her up, she sune cam' roun',
    (Ere lang the twa were man an' wife,)
But ne'er, whan dark, by Luggie burn
    She gaed as lang as she had life.

Mony a time the greetin' bairn,
   Whan it grew dark, an' late at nicht,
Gaed wailin' up an' doon the burn,
   An' mony gat an awfu' fricht.

The brutes, they say, aye sooner ken
   Whan some uncanny thing is near
Than man; an' aften start an' shy,
   An' turn, an' howl, an' sweat for fear.

My gutcher tauld when he was young,
   He an' his mate were on the spree;
" The wee short hour ayont the twal' "
   Had struck; an' they at hame maun be.

His brisk wee doggie ran before,
   An' aft ran back in gamesome mood,
Whan a' at ance a fearfu' howl
   He geid, an' like a stane he stood.

An' syne he turn'd him on his back,
   An' howl'd an' whin'd maist piteouslie:
The chiels in terror glour'd aroun',
   But no a leevin' thing cou'd see.

Wi' cowrin' heid, and clappit tail,
   He raise an' crawl'd their legs atween;
Frae there a fit he wadna steer:
   The lads were sairly fley'd, I ween.

A mile or twa they were frae hame,
    An' fast alang the road they sped ;
The dog ran cowrin' 'mang their feet,
    An' shook an' whined wi' fear an' dread.

They wan the door, an' drave it up,
    In sprang the dog before them baith,
An' gutcher said, "His name be prais'd
    Wha' fended us this nicht frae skaith ! "

He never gaed the bogle brae
    Again at witchin' time o' nicht :
An' but that nicht at Luggie burn
    He ne'er gat sic anither fricht.

Ye'll say that's juist an' aul' wife's tale,
    An' there's no ane believes it noo ;
Yet they were truthfu' honest folk
    Wha tauld the tale I tell to you.

GLOSSARY.

A

Ae, one.
Aiblins, perhaps, maybe.
Ain, own.
Air, early, soon.
Ait-farle, oatmeal cake.
Aften, often.
Aft, oft.
Afore, before.
Afiel', abroad, about.
Afterhen, afterwards.
Aff, off.
Ahint, behind.
Alloo'd, allowed.
Alack, alas.
Aneath, beneath.
Anent, in regard.
An', and.
Asteer, astir.
Ase, ashes.
Atween, between.
Aul', old.
Aughty, eighty.
Aumries, cupboards.
Auchts it, owns it.
Auld-farrant, far-seeing, knowing.
Ava', at all.
Awa', away.
Awsome, awful.

B

Bairn, child.
Bare the gree, bore the bell.
Baith, both.
Bauld, bold.
Bab, a bouquet.

Bardie, brisk, pert.
Bien, well-to-do.
Ben, in.
Belyve, betimes, by and by.
Beck, curtsey.
Beuk, book.
Bedicht, clothed.
Bedcral, church-officer or sexton.
Beet the fire, mend the fire.
Benison, blessing.
Beckin', basking.
Biel, shelter.
Bielin', covering.
Big-pouches, large pockets.
Biggin', building.
Bide, stop.
Bittock, a part.
Birrin', whirring.
Bizzin', buzzing.
Blithe, cheerful.
Blastit, blasted.
Blae, bluish, purple.
Blate, shy.
Blether'd, chattered.
Bleeze, Blaze.
Bogle, evil spirit.
Boud, bound, must.
Bow-wowin' tyke, barking dog.
Bout, about.
Boun', bound.
Bountith, bounty.
Boo, bow.
Boo'd, bowed.
Braid, broad.
Braws, bridal dresses, or finery.
Bracken, fern.
Breeks, small-clothes.
Broo, brow.

Bruck, brook, to approve, to bear.
Brocht, brought.
Brags, boasts.
Bricht, bright.
Braize, the roach.
Bracheid, top of an ascent.
Brent, smooth, broad, full.
Bruckle, brittle.
Busk, dress.
Burnie, brook, rivulet.
Bucklin' kame, comb for holding
  up the back hair.
Bummin', humming.
Byke, nest of wild bees or wasps.

C

Ca'd the pirns, filled the quills.
Cauld, cold.
Callan, a lad, a boy.
Carlin, an old woman.
Cam', came.
Ca', call.
Canty, merry.
Ca'd, called.
Canna, cannot.
Caum, calm.
Cantrip, charm, or spell.
Chips, little ones.
Chirmin', continuous, repeated,
  call.
Chitterin', shivering.
Chappie, young man.
Cheaterie, cheating.
Chap, knock.
Chiel', young fellow.
Chirtit, squeezed, pressed.
Chappit, knocked.
Clashes, gossip, tale-bearing.
Clour'd, battered.
Clockin', hatching.
Cleck, hatch.
Cleckit, hatched.
Cleedin', clothing.
Claver'se, Claverhouse.
Clout, piece of rag.
Clachan, village, hamlet.
Corncraik, landrail.

Corse, corpse.
Cog, a hooped wooden dish.
Cozie, comfortable.
Coom, soot.
Coo, cow.
Cosh, neat.
Contrair, contrary.
Cou'dna, could not.
Couthie, kindly.
Cot, small house.
Coorted, courted, wooed.
Coortin', wooing.
Cravin', asking, seeking.
Cranreuch, hoar-frost.
Craps, crops.
Crined, shrunk, shrivelled.
Craig, throat.
Crumpie, brittle.
Creepie, small, low stool.
Crack, talk.
Cries, banns.
Cried in kirk, banns proclaimed
  in church.
Cruzie, an open oil lamp.
Craw, rook, crow.
Cruse, bold, free.
Croon, low-singing, a crown.
Cuffed, boxed.
Cum, come.
Cutty, short pipe.
Cumin' roun', coming round.

D

Darn'd, pushed close in.
Dang, dashed.
Daurdna, durst not.
Dae, do.
Dautit, petted, made much of.
Daurin', daring.
Daffin', romping.
Deleerit, delirious, distracted.
Deid-ill, death-ill.
Deid, dead.
Dee't, died.
Dee, die.
Dinkit, well dressed.
Dichtet, wiped.

Didna, did not.
Dinilt, vibrated.
Dinna, do not.
Dirled, thrilled.
Dowie, listless, sad.
Dour, obstinate.
Douce, serious.
Dominie, schoolmaster.
Doun, down.
Donnert, stupid.
Dolefu', sorrowful.
Dolour, sorrow.
Downa, like not.
Doot, doubt.
Doo, dove.
Doun the brae, down the hill.
Droukit, drenched.
Drouth, thirst.
Droun, drown.
Dree, bear, suffer.
Dreed, suffered.
Dredour, dread.
Dreepin', dripping.
Dreigh, slow.
Drucken, drunken.
Dune, done.
Duntin', knocking, throbbing.
Dule, sorrow.
Duds, worn clothes.
Dwinin', falling off, growing less.
Dyke, hedge.

E

Ee, eye.
E'en, eyes, even.
E'nin's, evenings.
Eerie, fearful.
Eke, add, also.
Ekit, added, appended.
Eld, age, old.
Embro', Edinburgh.
Eneuch, enough.
Endoomintie, endowment.
Erles, earnest of something to come.
Ettlin', intending.

F

Fa', fate, fall.
Fain, fond.
Fautor, defaulter.
Fause, false.
Faund, found.
Fashous, troublesome.
Feydum, presentiment.
Feckless, worthless, weakly.
Feint, pretence.
Fen unco weel, fare very well.
Fen, tend, having enough.
Fecht, fight.
Feckly, mostly.
Fend, defend.
Firesum, five in number.
Fie, haste, shame.
Fitmarks, footprints.
Flichterin', fluttering.
Flyte, scold.
Flure, floor.
Fleyd, afraid.
Fock, folk, people.
Forfairn, desolate, forlorn.
Foursum, four in number.
Frae, from.
Freens, friends.
Fu', full.
Fule, fool.
Fyke, irritation.

G

Gae, go.
Gavel-en', gable-end.
Gars, compels.
Gane, gone.
Gaspit, gasped.
Gaed, went.
Galore, abundance, plenty.
Gate, road, way.
Gat, got.
Gang, go.
Garr'd, compelled.
Gabbie, talkative.
Gaun', going.
Gangin', walking.
Gash, well-to-do.
Gey, very.

Gear, money, goods.
Ghaist, ghost.
Gied, gave.
Gie, give.
Gi'en, given.
Girnel, large meal chest.
Gif, if.
Gill, dell or lane.
Girns, snarls.
Glintin', glancing.
Gloamin', twilight.
Glower'd, stared.
Glow'rin', staring.
Gleg, sharp, quick-sighted.
Gliff, surprise, fright.
Glunches, sulks, sulking.
Glaikit, careless, merriment.
Glib, sharp, knowing.
Glundy, sulky, sullen.
Gowden, golden.
Gowd, gold.
Goupin', throbbing.
Gowpen, the two hands joined and open.
Grumlin', grumbling.
Gree, agree.
Grip, hold.
Grit, great.
Grup, hold.
Greet, weep.
Greetin', weeping.
Grun', ground.
Grat, wept.
Groufs, bellies.
Graip, grope.
Grey-gate, evil-way.
Grippit, grasped.
Guidwull, goodwill.
Guff, puff.
Guid, good.
Gutcher, grandfather.
Gumption, common sense, quick-sighted.
Gully-knife, large knife.

H

Hauf, half.

Hackit feet. small hard cuts, from exposure to the weather.
Haud, hold.
Harn, coarse linen.
Ha'e, have.
Hale, whole.
Haunies, hands.
Haunie, handy.
Happit, covered.
Hantle, much, a good deal.
Haun', hand.
Hainin', sparing.
Haffitless, with a bonnet leaving the cheeks bare.
Hag, dry hollow in a moss.
Harl'd, trailed.
Hasp, hank of yarn.
Habble, hobbleshow, confusion.
Hauflins, half.
Hech, oh.
He'll, he will.
Het, hot.
Heid, head.
Heuks, hooks.
Herri't, ravaged, taken away.
Heezed, hoisted.
Hie, high.
Hinna, have not.
Hirsels, herds of cattle.
Hinny, honey.
Hirplin', crippling.
Hizzies, husseys, light-hearted, careless young women.
Houp, hope.
Howe. hollow.
Howkin', digging.
Hogger, old stocking without a foot.
Hoo, how.
Hoose, house.
Hughie, Hugh.
Hunner, hundred.

I

Ilka, every.
Ilk, each.
Ill-deedie, evil doing.

Ill-bedicht, poorly clad.
Ingle, fireside.
Inkling, slight knowledge.
I red, I warn.
I'se, I will, I shall.
I've, I have.
Ither, other.

J

Jaloose, suspect.
Jinkit, short, quick turns.
Jock, John.
Juist, just.
Jupe, a short-gown.

K

Kail-yard, kitchen-garden.
Kail, broth.
Kame, comb.
Ken, know.
Kenn'd, knew, known.
Kep, stop.
Kecked, looked.
Kirk, church.
Kin', kind.
Kintra, country.

L

Lawin', reckoning.
Laigh, low.
Laird, proprietor.
Lack, lose.
Lauch, laugh.
Lare, remainder, bathe with
water.
Lamiter, a lame person.
Leuk, look.
Leukit, looked.
Lea, leave, a grass field.
Leal-hertit, true-hearted.
Leev'd, lived.
Leeze me, dear to me, pleased with.
Lees, lies.
Leeve, live.
Leet, list.

Lift, sky.
Licht, light.
Liltit, sung.
Lippen, trust.
Listed, enlisted.
Loe, love.
Loch, lake.
Loed, loved.
Loupin', leaping.
Loesome, lovesome.
Lowsed, unyoked.
Lowe, flame, fire.
Loan, street.
Lozens, window panes.
Loon, false, worthless fellow.
Luntin', lighting, burning.
Lum, chimney.
Lug, ear.
Luif, palm of the hand.
Luve, love.
Linkin', walking quickly.

M

Marrow, one of two joined to-
gether, like another.
Maist-feck, most part.
Maun, must.
Mair, more.
Mane, moan.
Maistly, mostly.
Malison, malediction.
Maunna, must not.
Mensfu', well bred.
Meageries, mischances, troubles.
Mealtith, a meal.
Mirk, dark.
Micht, might.
Mowdies, moles, small animals
that burrow in the earth.
Mony, many.
Mony mae, many more.
Moilin', toiling.
Moolins, crumbs.
Muckle, large, much.
Mune, moon.
Mutchkin-stoup, pint measure.
Mutches, caps for women.

N

Nae mair, no more.
Nay-say, refusal, denial.
Na weel, not well.
Naething, nothing.
Nicht, night.
Neist owk, next week.
Neist, next.
Nocht, nothing. nought.
Nouther, neither.
Noo, now.

O

Ocht, ought.
Ony, any.
Owre, over.
Oot, out.
Oor, our.
Ootcome, upshot.
Owks, weeks.

P

Paidlin', paddling.
Pawkie, sly, cunning.
Pairt, part.
Parritch-pat, porridge-pot.
Pearlin's, lace frills.
Peat, piece of dry moss.
Pechin', puffing.
Pit, put.
Pine, regret, repine.
Pinch'd, scarcely able, straitened.
Pith, strength.
Pipet, frilled.
Pig, earthen pitcher.
Plenish't, plenished.
Plouts, plunges.
Pow, head.
Powther't, powdered.
Pocks, bags.
Poopit, pulpit.
Poortith, poverty.
Priggit, entreated, beseeched.
Pree, taste.
Pruved, proved.

Propine, a gift of gratitude.
Puir, poor.
Pu'd, pulled.
Pu'in', pulling.
Pykit, lean, fleshless.

Q

Quo', quoth, said.
Quat, quit.
Queer, strange, droll.
Queans, term of contempt for females.

R

Rase, rose.
Rashes, rushes.
Rave, tore.
Randy, a scold.
Red up, clear up.
Richt, right.
Rig, ridge.
Rin, run.
Rive an' rug, tear and pull.
Riff-raff, low, worthless.
Row't, rolled.
Rowin', rolling.
Rous'd, awakened, stirred up.
Rue, regret.
Rumilin', rumbling.

S

Saunted, sainted.
Sair, sore.
Sae, so.
Sall, shall.
Soften, soften.
Saum, psalm.
Saxteen, sixteen.
Sabbin', sobbing.
Sauld, sold.
Sackless, helpless, harmless.
Sark, shirt, shift.
Saughs, willows.
Schule, school.
Scaith, wrong, hurt.

Scad, shade, scald.
Scored, furrowed.
Screigh, scream, shriek.
Ser', serve.
Scrimply, scarcely, sparingly.
Sham, pretence.
Sheugh, ditch.
Shielin', shepherd's hut.
Shoogit, shook, quaked.
Shoon, shoes.
Shoolfu's, shovelfuls.
Sic, such.
Sinins, sinews.
Simmers, summers.
Skaith, harm.
Screigh o' day, dawn of day.
Skailed, dismissed from school.
Skelpin', running, scudding.
Skirl, scream.
Sleekit, smooth.
Slippit, by stealth, stealthily.
Slockened, quenched.
Smoor't, smothered.
Smeek, smoke.
Snell, sharp.
Sneck, latch.
Socht, sought.
Sodgers, soldiers.
Soun', sound.
Sowp, sup, a spoonful.
Speer, ask, inquire.
Spunkie, Will-o'-the-wisp, marsh
    fires.
Sprees, merry-makings.
Splore, uproar.
Spulzie, spoil.
Stanin', standing.
Stoun, throb of pain.
Stappit, stepped.
Stievely, stiffly.
Staun', stand.
Strang, strong.
Stran', strand.
Stude, stood.
Stap, step.
Stoun, surprise, pain.
Streek, stretch.
Streekit, stretched.

Stark an' strang, firm and strong.
Stachered, staggered.
Sta's, stalls.
Steerin', stirring.
Strack, struck.
Stacher, stagger.
Straikit, smoothed.
Studgel, stout, firm-built.
Stickit, stabbed.
Stank, stagnant pool or ditch.
Stour, dust.
Steer, stir.
Stance, place.
Stramash, disorder.
Stoiter, stumble.
Stell, still.
Stowsie, short, stout.
Sune, soon.
Swarft, fainted.
Swankie, tall, well-formed.
Swith, swift.
Swarfin', fainting.
Swallin', swelling.
Syne fu' an bien, then full and
    well stocked.
Syke, small watercourse.
Synin's, rinsings.
Syne, then.

T

Tauld, told.
Ta'en, taken.
Tackl't, inveigled.
Taes, toes.
Tak tent, take care.
Tatties, potatoes.
Tent, attend, care for.
Tentie, careful, kindly.
Tether'd, fastened to a stake by
    a rope.
Teuk, took.
Teddin', shedding.
Thae, those.
Thoosan's, thousands.
Thrangin', thronging.
Thochts, thoughts.
Thretty, thirty.

Thro'ither, merry, rollicking.
Thoom, thumb.
Theekit, thatched.
Tine, lose.
Tirlin', rapping.
Tint, lost.
Towmonds, twelvemonths.
Toddlin', tottering walk of a child.
Toun, town.
Tosh'd, trimmed, made neat.
Touzled, dishevelled.
Toom, empty.
Toom'd, emptied.
Tramped, trampled.
Trow, believe.
Trail'd, dragged.
Tremilt, trembled.
Trampers, travellers.
Twa, two.
'Tween between.
Twasum, two in number.
Twal-hoors, mid-day.

U

Unco, strange, very.
Unnerstude, understood.

V

Vogie, foppish.

W

Waesum, woeful.
Wadna, would not.
Wad, would.
Wa's, walls.
Wae, woe.
Warl', world.
Wabster, weaver.
Warkrife, industrious.
Wat-shod, tearful eyes, wet shoes.
Watna, don't know.
Wannert, wandered.
Warna, were not.
Wanworth, nominal, small price.
Wacfu' hap, woeful fate.
Wastlins, westlands.
Wallet, large bag.

Wasterie, careless waste.
Wame, belly.
Wag-at-the-wa', Dutch clock hanging at the wall.
Waesucks, woe for, sorry for.
Wallowt, faded.
We'll, we will.
Wearit, tired.
Wecht, a barn utensil.
Weeock, little while.
Ween, trow, think so.
Wee, small, little.
Whilk, which.
Whins, gorse.
Wheen, a quantity, a part.
Wha, who.
Whaur, where.
Whiles, sometimes.
Whistles to weet, to moisten the throats.
Wi', with.
Wile, entice.
Winnocks, windows.
Wierd, fate, fortune.
Wimplin', gliding.
Withootin, without any.
Wifie, wife.
Wizened, withered, wrinkled.
Win', wind.
Worrikow, goblin.
Wow, oh.
Woo', wool.
Wrocht, wrought.
Wrangs, wrongs.
Wull, will.
Wuds, woods.
Winna, will not.
Wyte, blame.
Wullcat, wildcat.

Y

Yaup, hungry.
Yestreen, yesternight, last night.
Yer, your.
Ye'se, you shall.
Yett, gate.
Yird, earth.
Yirth, earth.

"THE name of Janet Hamilton is one of the most remarkable in the history of Scottish poesy. That a woman in humble life —who did not enjoy the advantages of the usual elementary branches of a school education—should, at the age of 73, and while now blind, be capable of writing or composing verses at all, is singular enough ; but that these verses should possess the fervour, pathos, and genuine truthfulness of a Tannahill, and even—in all but his best pieces—of a Burns, can only be accounted for by the inheritance of genius. The ballad 'Effie,' for tenderness, simplicity, and beauty, deserves to be placed alongside of the immortal 'Auld Robin Gray' of Lady Ann Lindsay."—*Glasgow Daily Herald,* Nov. 28, 1868.

"Janet Hamilton is 73 years of age, and blind. The book now before us. however, needs no feeling of sympathy for the self-taught struggler to recommend it. It abounds in genuine poetry, which none but a richly-gifted and born poet could have produced."—*Evangelical Magazine,* April, 1869.

"Mrs. Janet Hamilton is a wonderful old lady. The first piece, entitled 'The Skylark Caged and Free,' is a piece of as genuine poetry as ever hatched itself and took wing since Homer sang."—*Evangelical Repository,* Dec., 1868.

"The 'Poems and Ballads' are instinct with insight, deep affection, and poetic genius."—*Forward,* Jan. 1, 1869.

"The 'Poems and Ballads' are distinguished by the power of versification, the graphic description, the shrewd sense, the sound moral tone, the humour, and pathos, and patriotic fire which have been so remarkable in her former productions. Many of the ballads are extremely touching."—*N. B. Daily Mail,* Dec. 7, 1868.

"Where there is poetic fire, it will appear. This fact we have illustrated in the poetry of Janet Hamilton."—*Ayrshire Express,* Nov. 28, 1868.

"Her ballads—such, for example, as the touching story of 'Effie'—are as remarkable for their fine feeling, and pathos, and true poetical flavour, as her Garibaldi addresses and her political songs are for their power and passion."—*Glasgow Morning Journal*, Dec. 5, 1868.

"Mrs. Hamilton is one of Nature's poets. Our Scotch brethren are, and have reason to be, proud of their female Burns."—*Christian Times*, London, Dec. 18, 1868.

"Janet Hamilton, we are sure, has no desire that her works should be judged by any other standard than those of their literary merits. Many of her poems are full of genuine poetic fire and feeling. 'Mary Lee' and the 'Monkland Martyr' are fine specimens of her ballad style. They are told with great simplicity and clearness, and contain lines of great poetic beauty."—*Hamilton Advertiser*, Dec. 5, 1868.

"The whole volume is one of the marvels of the age. That an old woman, 73 years of age, should indite such gems—so vivid in fancy, so rich in imagery, so powerful in delineation, and so elevated in tone and sentiment—is beyond all doubt a marvel."—*Northern Ensign*, Dec. 10, 1868.

"In this new volume we are so pleased with the poetry that we lose ourselves amid its profusion of beauties, and have an instinctive conviction that Janet Hamilton is a poet of God's own making—as all true poets are—and that she sings because she cannot help it. We have found the volume abounding in excellence and beauty, and have been unable to detect an objectionable line in the whole book."—*Airdrie Advertiser*, Dec. 5, 1868.

"Sweet and clear natural notes of an untrained muse. Janet Hamilton is a true poetess. Her ballads and songs are for liberty and truth; and, therefore, far let their notes ring forth."—*Sword and Trowel*, C. H. SPURGEON, Jan., 1869.

"We almost lose sight of the intrinsic value of this book—which is very great—by the remarkable circumstances connected with its author. Self-taught, poor, and now blind and old, Janet Hamilton adds fresh lustre to the literary fame of Scotland."—*Evangelical Magazine and Missionary Chronicle*, London, May, 1869.

"In the poems which compose this volume she has shown poetic genius of a superior order. Some of the pieces possess great merit for their beauty and force of expression, and others, in homely Doric numbers, have a tender pathos and power that must thrill every Scottish heart."—*United Presbyterian Magazine*, Jan., 1869.

"Janet Hamilton is altogether an original and (like Homer) a self-taught poet. She has written a volume of poems full of tenderness and power, instinct with true genius baptised by religion."—*Methodist New Connexion Magazine*, London, Feb., 1869.

"Scotland can boast of poets of rich natural genius—in Burns, Scott, and others—to whom must be added Janet Hamilton. Many of her verses remind us of the fire and genius of Burns, and

like him—being self-taught—her effusions bear the mark of freshness that originality and true poetic fervour can alone impart.
Some of the pathetic pieces depict many of the finest feelings of
our nature."—*The Bookseller*, London, March 1, 1869.

"The poems contained in this book are vocal with the music
of Nature. You hear the rippling of the stream, the moaning of
the blast, and the roar of the ocean—you smell the perfume of
the 'fragrant birch and scented briar.'"—*Primitive Church or
Baptist Magazine*, London, Jan., 1869.

"It may be long before the public, and especially the public of
Scotland, shall again meet with the pathos, tenderness, humour,
good sense, and poetic *vis* abounding in the pages of Janet
Hamilton."—*Sabbath School Magazine*, April, 1869.

"Janet Hamilton is pre-eminently a poet of social progress.
Elizabeth Barrett Browning never penned a more piercing 'Cry
of the Human,' or a more urgent 'Cry of the Children,' than
Janet has done in some of her own spirit-stirring utterances."—
Our Own Fireside Magazine, London. Nov., 1869.

"Janet Hamilton's poetry is of the ballad style, and exceedingly simple—coming sweet, unrestrained, and felicitous as the
song of a bird. She has the simplicity, indeed, that Coleridge
and Wordsworth lauded and strove after, and which is the characteristic of the finest lyrics."—*North of England Advertiser*,
Dec. 5, 1868.

"Of Janet Hamilton as a poet we need have no fear in affirming
that, in certain respects common to both, there is no Scottish
bard since Robert Burns can be named alongside of her in power
of delineating Scottish life, and in her command alike of her
native Doric; and in 'the well of English undefiled' she appears
to us to approach Burns more nearly than any other poet of her
own home-born class."—*League Journal*, Dec. 19, 1868.

"The volume displays great power of delineation and much
tenderness of feeling. All the pieces are marked by a deep religious feeling and a refined taste, and will have special charms for
those who appreciate nature and natural description."—*The Freeman*, London, Dec. 18, 1868.

"The difficulty is what to quote, for there is so much that is
sweet and fine; and that, after being once read, will often be
read again, until some of the couplets find the way into the
memory."—*Dumfries Herald and Register*, Dec. 18, 1868.

"Those familiar with Anacreon's 'Ode to Spring' will see
how the poetic mind catches the same broad features of nature.
'The Watercoot among the Rushes' (Janet Hamilton's) is the
counterpart of the Greek lyrist's 'Duck Swimming in the Waters.'
Place the 'Ode' alongside of the poem before us, and we feel
assured the latter will not suffer by the comparison."—*Daily
Review*, Edinburgh, Dec. 21, 1868.

"It is in domestic scenes—in their manifold relations and

divergences—that Janet Hamilton supremely and shiningly sits as Poetic Queen."—*Hawick Advertiser,* Dec. 26, 1868.

"One noticeable circumstance pleasant to us is its rich and delicious Scottish dialect, and an amount of poetic sensibility truly extraordinary." — *The Eclectic,* London, Dec., 1868.

"In the present volume we find a further illustration 'of the truth of that remark, ' Were all poets classically educated, it might be better for the poets, but to a very large degree it would be worse for their poetry.' When Scotland reckons up her poets, the name of Janet Hamilton will not be forgotten."—*Illustrated Times,* London, Dec. 26, 1868.

"Some of her pieces glow with political fervour, while others have been inspired by the beauties of natural scenery, and at times there is a gentle sweetness in the aged singer's voice."— *Literary World,* London. Jan. 1, 1869.

"Mrs. Hamilton is a true Scotch pebble, reflecting in miscellaneous broken lights and shadows the emotions and aspirations of a genuine poetic heart. She touches many strings ; but she shows to most advantage in ballad, of which one, called ' Effie,' affords ample proof ; and in her other pieces she delights to show the colour of her politics by raining thunderbolts on all tyrants and tyrannies, whether physical or moral."—*London Review,* Jan. 2, 1869.

"This is an edition of wonderful old Janet Hamilton's poems. Many of them are graceful and pathetic ; many more vigorous ; and the volume is well worth buying."— *London Quarterly Review,* April, 1869.

"Her verses show a good eye for natural objects, and for character, kindly sympathy, and a sense of humour. They are also in good taste—often elegant. It is no common delicacy of perception, no common feeling for natural tenderness, which has inspired some of her lines."— *The Nonconformist,* London, Feb. 17, 1869.

"Janet Hamilton is no lackadaisical poetess. There is nerve and backbone in all her utterances : but there is no hardness in her nature. She vibrates like a poplar leaf to the faintest breeze of real emotion. It is only your sham sentiment which she drives through as a herd laddie does a gossamer on the whin bushes. Nor is she ever insincere. We feel the pulse beating with the blood-throb from the full heart—not the methodical and laboured stroke of the sentiment pump."—*The London Scotsman,* Jan. 2, 1869.

"We might commend the book as the production of a senior of 73, never gifted with educational or conventional advantages, and now laden with the double burden of blindness and years, but we prefer to rest its claims upon its own literary merit, which is great, and upon the character of its author, which is nobler still." —*The City Press,* London, Jan. 9, 1869.

"In simple ballads, in episodes of feeling which touch the

heart's finest chords, and in painting the moral heroisms of domestic life. our authoress has few equals, and hardly any superior."—*The Londonderry Standard.* Jan. 16, 1869.

"There is a deep pathos and considerable poetic beauty in the ballads ; and in the pieces generally there is that indescribable touch of genius expressive of the true poet."—*Social Reformer,* Feb. 1, 1869.

"Janet Hamilton first snatched the divine fire from 'Paradise Lost' and Allan Ramsay's Poetical Works. These books she happened to find upon a weaver's loom when she was but in her eighth year."—*The Budget,* London, Nov. 28, 1868.

"The subjects of Janet's poems are always massive and substantial. The lover of the true Doric of old Scotland will find a rich treat in this volume, the most striking and apt expressions of which become as ductile in her hands as a thread of gold."— *The Presbyterian Witness,* Halifax, U.S., Feb. 13, 1869.

EXTRACTS FROM PRIVATE LETTERS.

From Mrs. H. B. Stowe.—"Hartford County, 23rd June, 1869. Dear Mrs. Hamilton,—I thank you for your kindness in sending me your volume of charming poems. I was much interested in your poem, 'The Old Graveyard.' I think in some parts it is equal to Gray's 'Elegy.'—S. H. B. STOWE."

From late Rev. Dr. Guthrie, Edinburgh, to a Private Friend.— "Some of Janet's poetry is worthy of Burns, and some of her prose worthy of Hugh Miller. I could not say more."

From Lord Houghton to the Authoress.—"You have illustrated the proposition that I maintained in Edinburgh, that good composition in prose is always sure to go with good composition in verse."

From Lord Shaftesbury to the Authoress.—"I have read many of your pieces with great delight, for their noble and tender spirit and the true piety that pervades all their elegance."

From Professor Blackie, Edinburgh, to the Authoress.—"I have read and enjoyed not a few of your pieces. They are full of a vigorous health and natural spirit—sunny and fresh, like the breeze that sweeps o'er a heather brae on a sunny day."

AIRD AND COGHILL, PRINTERS, GLASGOW.

www.ingramcontent.com/pod-product-compliance
Lightning Source LLC
Chambersburg PA
CBHW021212270326
41929CB00010B/1094